DAVID HARE

Racing
Demon

faber and faber

First published in 1990
by Faber and Faber Limited
3 Queen Square London WC1N 3AU
First revised edition published in 1991
This second revised edition published in 1996

Photoset by Parker Typesetting Service Leicester
Printed and bound in Great Britain by
Mackays of Chatham PLC, Chatham, Kent

A CIP record for this book is available
from the British Library

ISBN 0-571-16106-5

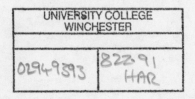
13 15 17 19 20 18 16 14 12

For Blair

Why, who makes much of a miracle?
I know of nothing else but miracles.

WALT WHITMAN

CHARACTERS

Clergy

THE REV LIONEL ESPY

THE RT REV CHARLIE ALLEN, BISHOP OF SOUTHWARK

THE REV TONY FERRIS

THE REV DONALD 'STREAKY' BACON

THE REV HARRY HENDERSON

THE RT REV GILBERT HEFFERNAN, BISHOP OF KINGSTON

Laity

FRANCES PARNELL

STELLA MARR

HEATHER ESPY

EWAN GILMOUR

TOMMY ADAIR

Waiters, Synod members, etc.

Racing Demon was first performed by the National Theatre Company at the Cottesloe at the National Theatre, London on 8 February 1990. The cast was as follows:

THE REV. LIONEL ESPY	Oliver Ford Davies
THE RT REV CHARLIE ALLEN	Richard Pasco
FRANCES PARNELL	Stella Gonet
THE REV TONY FERRIS	Adam Kotz
STELLA MARR	Joy Richardson
THE REV DONALD 'STREAKY' BACON	David Bamber
THE REV HARRY HENDERSON	Michael Bryant
HEATHER ESPY	Barbara Leigh-Hunt
EWAN GILMOUR	Ewan Stewart
TOMMY ADAIR/HEAD WAITER/SERVER	Paul Moriarty
THE RT REV GILBERT HEFFERNAN	Malcolm Sinclair
WAITER/SERVER	Andrew Woodall
Director	Richard Eyre
Décor	Bob Crowley
Lighting	Mark Henderson
Music	George Fenton

I want to acknowledge the generous help and advice given to me by members of the Church of England during the writing of this play. Any inauthenticity is wholly my fault.

DH

ACT ONE

SCENE ONE

REVEREND LIONEL ESPY *is kneeling on the ground. He is in his fifties with a bald head fringed with white hair. He wears a black cassock. He is addressing God.*

LIONEL: God. Where are you? I wish you would talk to me. God. It isn't just me. There's a general feeling. This is what people are saying in the parish. They want to know where you are. The joke wears thin. You must see that. You never say anything. All right, people expect that, it's understood. But people also think, I didn't realize when he said *nothing*, he really did mean absolutely nothing at all. You see, I tell you, it's this perpetual absence – yes? – this not being here – it's that – I mean, let's be honest – it's just beginning to get some of us down. You know? Is that unreasonable? There are an awful lot of people in a very bad way. And they need something beside silence. God. Do you understand?

SCENE TWO

The garden of Southwark's palace. SOUTHWARK *is in his sixties, a tall laconic figure, his black hair pressed against his skull. He is leading* LIONEL *out of the house into the garden.*

SOUTHWARK: Lionel, it's always such a pleasure to see you.
LIONEL: What a wonderful smell.
SOUTHWARK: Indeed. My wife always fries her fishcakes in duck fat. It's not just the taste. It improves the texture as well.
LIONEL: Goodness.
SOUTHWARK: It's funny, yesterday, you know, we had the salmon. And there's no denying poached salmon's very nice. But all the time I was thinking, when do we get the fishcakes?
LIONEL: Ah yes.
(LIONEL *stands a moment, waiting.*)

SOUTHWARK: Same with lamb. A leg of lamb is also very nice. But isn't the whole point that next day you have shepherd's pie?

LIONEL: Yes. Yes, well I know what you mean.

(LIONEL *waits, confused. But* SOUTHWARK *seems oblivious*.)

SOUTHWARK: And your wife? Heather? She cooks?

LIONEL: Yes. Yes, frequently.

SOUTHWARK: Good.

(SOUTHWARK *looks at him a moment*.)

Lionel, I suspect you sense the reason for this meeting . . .

LIONEL: No, tell me.

SOUTHWARK: We go back a very long way. After all, your whole family . . . Your father instructed me at Cuddesdon . . . Your uncles . . . your brother . . . where is he?

LIONEL: Mombasa.

SOUTHWARK: Your grandfather, Dean of St Paul's. He stood on the steps watching the bombs fall. Espy is one of the great clerical names. But I have had rumour of some stirrings among your parishioners.

(*A pause*.)

It's difficult, Lionel.

LIONEL: Please. You must tell me why.

SOUTHWARK: There is an element in your parish which is unsure of you. They've begun to doubt you. Maybe question the power of your convictions.

LIONEL: Anything specific?

SOUTHWARK: Extremely specific. They're not sure you still believe in the rules of the club.

(LIONEL *looks at him a moment*.)

I don't mean to upset you.

LIONEL: What parishioners are these? It's a largely working-class parish. They are my ministry. I don't have to tell you, Charlie, Christ came to help the poor.

SOUTHWARK: I know your views.

LIONEL: But there is, I know, a small middle-class rump . . .

SOUTHWARK: Not that small . . .

LIONEL: A rump of regular communicants who've been coming to the church for a very long time . . .

SOUTHWARK: They have.

2

LIONEL: And since the poor are not given to visiting bishops' palaces, I assume the complaint is from them?

(*He looks, but* SOUTHWARK *doesn't answer.*)

All right, you can't say . . .

SOUTHWARK: They're not very happy.

LIONEL: Why don't they come to me?

SOUTHWARK: Something in your manner?

LIONEL: Oh really?

SOUTHWARK: Yes.

(*He takes a look at* LIONEL, *but* LIONEL *is deadpan.*)

We are talking about the way you conduct the service of Communion. This is the problem. It's only an impression, nothing more. I do have to ask you if you're still interested in the sacramental side of your work.

(*There is a short pause.*)

LIONEL: Sometimes I'm impatient . . .

SOUTHWARK: Uh-huh . . .

LIONEL: Perhaps there are times when that comes across.

SOUTHWARK: I'm afraid it does.

LIONEL: You know the situation. It is fairly desperate. In our area I wouldn't even say the Church was a joke. It's an irrelevance. It has no connection with most people's lives. A lot of people are struggling to make a life at all. Now I feel we should be humble about this. Our job is mainly to listen and to learn. From ordinary, working people. We should try to understand and serve them. (*Shrugs slightly.*) Perhaps, with time, I do find that more important than ritual.

SOUTHWARK: Yes. Can the two be divided like that? (*Looks at him beadily, his manner changing.*) After all, what are we? Lionel? What is the Anglican Communion? It's a very loose church. I don't have to tell you, we all agree on very little. Almost nothing. Start talking to our members and you'll find we hold a thousand different views. Only one thing unites us. The administration of the sacrament. (*Pauses a moment.*) Finally that's what you're there for. As a priest you have only one duty. That's to put on a show.

(LIONEL *is looking at him thoughtfully.*)

LIONEL: Do you really think that?

SOUTHWARK: Doesn't matter what I think. Does it? That's the

wonderful thing. We're not talking about opinion. We're talking about authority. History. What the Church of England *is*. It's a disparate body held together by a common liturgy.

(LIONEL *looks at him mistrustfully, deciding how frank to be.*)

LIONEL: Charlie, to me, Christ is in our actions. Don't you think some of this other stuff just puts people off?

(SOUTHWARK *looks satisfied, as if he's got to the heart of it. Then he shrugs.*)

SOUTHWARK: Well, there you are. That's your opinion. However, the fact is, you are a priest. Give Communion. Hold services. Offer the full liturgy. And look cheerful as you do it. The people you call middle class are entitled to that. I don't call them any class. I call them believers. And, as you observed, there are all too few of those. So please . . . let's not be careless of them. (*He is suddenly quiet.*) It seems to me they're entitled to a little respect. (*Waits a moment.*) For the rest, by all means, come and discuss your views with me. Happy to. I do it all the time. With all sorts. But, meanwhile, please, fulfil your job description. Keep everyone happy.

(*There's a pause.*)

There. I've said it. (*Calls from his chair, not moving.*) Beatrice! (*Turns back.*) Now we'll have lunch.

SCENE THREE

Frances's living room. A flat in South London. FRANCES PARNELL *is thirty, blonde. She is lying on the floor, covered by a sheet.* THE REV TONY FERRIS *is younger than she is, sitting on a hard chair, at the end of the sheet. He has a loose-fitting modern suit, and a dog collar. He has wavy black hair and a fresh, open face.*

FRANCES: What happened then?
TONY: Oh, you know. Have I never told you?
FRANCES: No.

(*They both smile.*)

TONY: I was just a boy from the provinces. This was my first trip to London. I was only sixteen. I was incredibly lonely. I was thinking, all right, I'm frightened, I'm on my own, what would help would be if I could buy a small crucifix. This was in Oxford Street. There was a gift shop. I talked to the girl behind the counter. 'I think I've seen one,' she said. She seemed a bit puzzled. So she went into the back. Then when she came out, she had a couple. She said, 'Oh, I don't think you'll want this one. It's got a little man on it.'

FRANCES: Yes.

(*They laugh.*)

That's funny.

TONY: I mean, where had she been all her life? (*He looks down at her a moment.*) Are you going to get dressed?

FRANCES: (*Smiles.*) If you like. Does it make you uncomfortable?

TONY: No.

FRANCES: You always dress first.

TONY: Lot to do.

FRANCES: Do you have time for a pizza?

TONY: If you hurry.

(*She gets up, gathering the sheet around her. She goes out to change.* TONY *is thoughtful, not moving from his chair. He calls through to the bedroom.*)

TONY: It's just tonight I want to work on a scheme I have. Which I want to put to the team. I've got an idea for common worship, to try and involve the Catholics and Methodists as well. I wanted to start with a day for World Peace. Or something. If we could get everyone together it would be the most incredible coup. It would really . . .

(FRANCES *has come back in. She has pulled on jeans and a shirt.* TONY *stops speaking when she re-appears, as if censoring himself.*)

FRANCES: What?

TONY: No, then I think we'd really get people talking. Christ would be bang in the centre of things.

(FRANCES *moves across the room and gets a hair-brush. She starts brushing her hair.* TONY, *still in his chair, looks down.*)

I'm sorry.

FRANCES: No.

TONY: I can tell what you're thinking.

5

FRANCES: It's always Christ. We're alone. We make love. We have a little time. (*Smiles.*) And then Christ enters the room.

TONY: Yes. Well he's there. He's always with us.

FRANCES: I always pretend you're no different from anyone else. But you are. You always bring your friend to the party.

TONY: I can't help it.

FRANCES: I know.

(*They both smile. She crosses the room to put her coat on, easily running her hand across his back as she goes.*)

And is he coming for a pizza?

TONY: Inevitably.

FRANCES: And will be staying here tonight?

TONY: He will. But I can't.

FRANCES: Oh really?

TONY: No. Didn't I mention my aunt's coming down?

(*She looks at him a moment.*)

FRANCES: No. You forgot.

TONY: Yes. Aunt Ethel. She's ridiculously proud of me. I think she'd have preferred a nice smart parish in Surrey. But I explained I had to have the challenge of somewhere really difficult.

FRANCES: And when's she coming?

TONY: Oh, you know. This evening.

FRANCES: Mmm.

(*She stands a moment, her coat on. She's ready to go.* TONY *doesn't get up.*)

TONY: It's getting rather late for my meeting. I think I'll skip the pizza. Do you mind?

FRANCES: How long have you been here? Forty-five minutes?

TONY: Yes. I'm sorry. (*Looks down again.*) It's very wrong.

(*She looks at him a moment, then starts to move away.*)

FRANCES: Well, certainly it doesn't make me feel very valued . . .

TONY: I know.

FRANCES: Is Aunt Ethel really coming?

TONY: Why do you say that?

FRANCES: Because I can tell when you're lying.

(TONY *is very subdued.*)

6

TONY: Yes. Tomorrow she is.

(FRANCES *is very still*.)

TONY: Look, I'm sorry . . .

FRANCES: It's all right. I don't want an explanation.

TONY: No, really.

FRANCES: I'd rather not. It'll be humiliating. For both of us.

TONY: I'm going to feel rotten. In fact I do feel rotten already. Unless you let me share what I think. (*Waits, but she says nothing.*) I mean, I know this sounds terrible, but the fact is, our relationship . . . well, *we* understand. It's a caring and loving relationship, with some eventual purpose. It's in the context of . . . well, of our future. Of one day marrying. I mean we've sort of joked about it. But I think that's what we've both thought. Haven't we? (*He pauses. She doesn't answer.*) I mean, you know I would *never* . . . the physical experience, I mean you understand it's always in the context of a long-term commitment. An idea, if you like. Which both of us have. And which is terribly exciting.

FRANCES: But?

(*He looks at her mistrustfully.*)

TONY: But I have been getting worried how it may look to the rest of the world. (*Gets up quickly to stifle her reaction.*) I mean, you know I don't have any hang-ups. Personally. The biblical evidence is pretty inconclusive. We all know. We have advanced. Paul wasn't Jesus. You can read the Bible either way. All that so-called Christian morality, we understand it can be too narrowly interpreted. It's a question of what feels right in your heart. And with you it's always felt right. I promise you. I believe in the expression of God's love through another human being. In a serious context, it's good. But lately I don't know . . . it's made me uneasy.

FRANCES: Uneasy in yourself?

TONY: Yes. Partly.

FRANCES: Or uneasy for what the Bishop might say?

TONY: (*Indignant*) You know that's not fair.

FRANCES: Isn't it? I can see you're frightened. I'm not sure why. Either it's your conscience, or else you just don't want to get caught.

7

(*Walks across the room and gets his raincoat.*) You'd better go.
You'll be late for your meeting.

TONY: I can't go.

FRANCES: Why not?

TONY: Don't be ridiculous. I've told you my side. I've tried to
communicate my thoughts.

FRANCES: Well, you have.

TONY: But what do you think?

FRANCES: Nothing. (*Shakes her head.*) Honestly, I have nothing
to say.

(TONY *stands. He is gentle now.*)

TONY: Frances. Please say.

FRANCES: What does it matter? You've come this far without
talking to me. It had to be dragged from you as it was. I feel
I'm no longer even part of this. You've started not to look at
me. Aren't I irrelevant? Aren't you in an argument with
God? (*Hands across his coat.*) Here's your coat. (*Stops, close to
him now.*) And look – for the record – I didn't make love in
any 'context'. Whatever that may mean. I made love because
I wanted you. Is that really such a terrible idea?

(*He smiles, a warmth suddenly reappearing between them.*)
I liked your innocence. You came up from Bristol, you were
a Christian. All right, I got over that. Because your faith was
fresh. It was simple. You managed to be a normal person as
well. Yes, well exactly. It's a high compliment. After my
childhood. (*Turns away.*) But it's over.

TONY: No, Frances. I'm not saying that.

FRANCES: No, I am. You've got the bug. I've seen it before.
(*Shakes her head, quiet now.*) All you want is to carry the
Cross.

TONY: Not at all. Look, it's just . . . it's terribly complicated. It's
team ministry. There are three churches. We try to minister
to the whole area's needs. It is very exciting. It's also
demanding. So anything that . . . (*Pauses, disastrously.*)

FRANCES: That what?

TONY: I don't know how to put this . . . anything that dissipates
my energy . . .

(FRANCES *is suddenly furious.*)

FRANCES: I think you should definitely leave.

8

(*But* TONY *rides in on top of her, confronting her at last.*)

TONY: It was exciting. It was wonderful. You know. All through
ordination. No question, it was you who got me through.
After everything. In every way, it was such a tough time. 'Am
I worthy? Am I really up to it? Fulfilling God's mission on
earth?' I found being with you in the evening was restful. It
seemed natural. Just to walk on the common. Listen to your
office gossip. All that advertising stuff. Not thinking about
theology. But it's got harder since then. (*Looks at her
anxiously.*) I've got frightened of drift. I want to be
purposeful. Look where we're working. It's nowhere, it isn't
Brixton, it isn't even Kennington. Basically it's just a horrid
great road surrounded by council estates. With thousands of
people whose lives could be infinitely richer. It's my job to
give them some sense of joy. How can I get on with it unless
. . . unless my own private life is sort of cleared out the way?
(*She just looks at him.*)
At the moment it's messy. When I wake up, I think, today's
the day I shall see her. Of course I'm thrilled. But also I feel a
kind of dread. It raises questions. It's a feeling in my stomach.
(*Shakes his head.*) I'm not sure I can afford that any more.
(FRANCES *is very quiet.*)

FRANCES: No.

TONY: You've been so good for me. You know I'll always want to
be friends.

FRANCES: Why is there one word you're frightened to use?

TONY: Which one? (*Frowns.*) What word?

FRANCES: I'm not a Christian, so it doesn't frighten me.

TONY: I have no idea what you mean.

FRANCES: (*Smiles*) The word is sin. Why don't you use it? You've
been sinning.
(*He looks at her, silenced.*)
Well, isn't that what you think?

SCENE FOUR

*Lionel's sitting room in a Victorian terraced house in South London. At
one end* STELLA MARR *is sitting by herself on a hard chair. She is black,*

9

*in her mid-twenties. She is in evident distress. She sits a moment,
waiting. Then* LIONEL *comes in carrying a box of tissues, which he
offers gently to her.*

LIONEL: I brought you these.

STELLA: Oh, thank you.

*(She takes one. He stoops down and puts the box on the floor
beside her.)*

LIONEL: I'll put them there. They're beside you. Now please tell
me what happened next.

(She waits a moment, recovering, then starts.)

STELLA: Well after I got out, I was feelin' terrible. So I started
takin' these pills.

LIONEL: Who gave them to you?

STELLA: A doctor. I dunno. I never seen 'im again.

LIONEL: The same doctor?

STELLA: Oh no. I din' never meet that doctor.

*(*LIONEL *nods.)*

LIONEL: I see.

STELLA: They just let you in, there's a nurse, and then they
knock you out. Then you wake up and it's over. 'Cept for me
it wa'n't.

LIONEL: What do you mean?

STELLA: I 'ad to 'ave another one. They 'en't done a proper
scrape.

LIONEL: Uh-huh. *(Pauses again, waiting.)* Where was this?

STELLA: Lewisham. I din' understand it. They said they couldn'
find it. So they 'ad to take another look.

LIONEL: Yes. How long between the two?

STELLA: Oh, it was a Monday. Monday's the slow day, it's the
only day they'll let me off. *(Beginning to cry again.)* So it was
Monday, then Monday.

LIONEL: I see. Two Mondays.

STELLA: We 'ad to pay twice.

LIONEL: Who paid?

STELLA: My 'usband. 'E got money. 'E jus' din' wanna 'ave kids.
(Crying now.) The second Monday they found it, then they
threw it away.

*(*LIONEL *watches.)*

I might 'ave coped, you know. 'Cept 'e gets so angry. Now I cry all the time. That's what drives 'im mad. 'E says, will you never stop cryin'? An' I say, I'd like to, I can't.

LIONEL: Can you go somewhere else? Do you want to leave him?

STELLA: I a'n't got no money. I've nowhere to go. (*Looks at him now.*) What does the Church say?

LIONEL: What does it say? About abortion? (*Pauses a moment, very quiet.*) Abortion is wrong. (*Then he looks at her, unapologetic.*)

STELLA: I couldn' 'elp it.

LIONEL: I know. I'm not saying *you* were wrong. You had no choice.

STELLA: I don' wanna leave him.

LIONEL: I know. And also it's a marriage. We want your marriage to last. Is there a chance your husband might come in and see me?

(*She looks at him mistrustfully.*)

It's a stupid question, I'm sorry.

STELLA: I told my friend at work, she said, why go and see a vicar? You don' even know 'im. What can 'e do?'

(*TONY appears at the door, surprised LIONEL's not alone.*)

TONY: Oh Lionel, am I interrupting?

LIONEL: Tony, it's all right.

(*But STELLA has already begun to get up.*)

We're just going to pray.

STELLA: (*Alarmed*) What?

LIONEL: Shut your eyes.

(*He closes his own, leaving her with no choice. TONY does too.*)

LIONEL: O God, who understands everything, please be good to Stella here. She needs love. Make her pain less and give her the strength to bear it. Through Jesus Christ our Lord. Amen.

TONY: Amen.

(*They open their eyes. There is a short, charmed silence, like a spell.*)

STELLA: Will that help?

LIONEL: I don't know. It can't do any harm.

(*He gets up to say goodbye to her.*)

I'll call by your salon. I haven't much hair. But you can cut
it.

STELLA: Oh, I only wash.

LIONEL: Yes, I'm sorry. I wish I had more.

(*He fingers the fringe at the back of his head. Then takes her
hand.*)

I don't know if God'll help you. But now you do have a
friend. You have me. This house is always open. Whenever
you're lonely.

STELLA: Oh, I see. Is that it?

LIONEL: Yes. (*Nods.*) That is the service.

STELLA: Oh. (*Stands a moment, uncertain.*) Well, thanks very
much.

(*He smiles at her as she leaves. Then turns his attention to the
piles of duplicated papers on the table.*)

LIONEL: Tony, hello, I apologize, the clock overtook me.

TONY: What was all that about?

(LIONEL *throws him a brief disapproving look.*)

LIONEL: Will you give me a hand? I've cyclostyled all this stuff.

TONY: Sorry. Breach of confidence.

(*But he doesn't move to help* LIONEL *with all the paperwork. He
waits.*)

It's none of my business. I'm just interested. I've been
thinking a lot about how we handle things. Did you know
her?

LIONEL: No.

TONY: Is she a churchgoer?

LIONEL: I wouldn't think so. She just dropped by for help.

(TONY *nods.* LIONEL *works, sorting papers into piles.*)

TONY: I mean, I don't know what you'd been saying before I
came in.

(LIONEL *starts stapling A4 sheets together.* TONY *watches.*)

I tell you, it just occurred to me . . . I could see she was in
distress.

LIONEL: She'd had a very bad experience.

TONY: You did say a prayer, but it was very low key.

LIONEL: Yes.

TONY: No, my question is . . . I know the theory, I know the
theory of 'Let them come to you', 'don't judge' . . .

LIONEL: That's right.

TONY: But is it deliberate you never mention the Bible at all?

LIONEL: If I give her a Bible, her husband will find it. If he finds out she's been to see me, he'll get even more hostile. The marriage is in trouble already. We don't want to make it worse by making him feel the do-gooders are all ganging up on him.

TONY: Goodness. (*Nods*.) You have to think of everything.

LIONEL: Yes. You'll get used to it.

TONY: So what will happen to her?

LIONEL: I don't know. (*Turns hopelessly*.) I can call the social services. You know the mess they're in. And to say what? There's a young woman hooked on antidepressants who's living in fear of her husband? You know what they'll say: 'So what else is new?' Or else they'll refer her to a doctor. Well it's the doctors who gave her the pills. All they'll do now is refer her to someone like me. And so on. For ever.

TONY: Lionel, isn't it . . . I'm just asking the question . . . isn't this the perfect moment to tell her about Christ?

(LIONEL *turns and looks at him, as if for the first time really taking him in*.)

Look, please don't think I'm interfering . . .

LIONEL: Not at all . . .

TONY: I'm not. But you're the team Rector. Do we need a team policy?

LIONEL: I'm not sure.

TONY: To deal with exactly this kind of case?

LIONEL: Stella's not a case. She's a person.

TONY: Naturally.

LIONEL: And there's something distasteful in what you're suggesting. I don't approve of cashing in on people's unhappiness. It's very dangerous, because someone is in grief to think, 'Oh, good.' We're not salesmen. We don't look at people's suffering and think, 'Oh, this is excellent, now we've got a foot in the door.'

(*He looks at* TONY, *now checking the vehemence of his tone*.)

Whatever we are, we're not ambulance chasers. If the need is there, it will show.

TONY: But what if it doesn't? I mean, what are we telling her?

LIONEL: I'm not telling her anything. I'm just hoping she'll come back. Perhaps when her husband's more rational. And then one day she'll find life is easier with a religious dimension. (*Sits down, his papers in front of him. Then, quietly.*) Or, on the other hand, maybe she won't.

(TONY *is looking at him, shocked, when they are interrupted by* THE REV DONALD 'STREAKY' BACON. *He is in his early forties, in a duffel coat with bright orange reflector pads and bicycle clips. He also carries bicycle knapsacks. He is very cheerful and outgoing, in glasses and with a thick shock of hair.*)

STREAKY: Hello!

LIONEL: Hello, Streaky.

STREAKY: Can somebody tell me? Aren't cyclists people? Hello, Tony. (*Bends down to remove his clips.*) That's why I'm late.

LIONEL: You cycled in the rush hour? You're crazy.

STREAKY: Lorries behave as if you don't exist. It's like going down a canyon. High wall on that side, high wall on the other . . .

TONY: I wonder, do you mind if I say . . .

(LIONEL *looks up, catching this, but* STREAKY *is taking his knapsacks off and putting them on the table, oblivious.*)

STREAKY: I could have been deaded. Like Neddy Seagoon. Or was it Bluebottle who was deaded? I can never remember.

LIONEL: (*Quiet, authoritative*) It wasn't Neddy Seagoon.

TONY: I'm sorry, Streaky . . .

(STREAKY *stops, realizing he has interrupted something.*)

It's just you walked in right in the middle of things.

STREAKY: Oh lawks, have I really? Is this the meeting? Did you start without me? Where's Harry?

(*In comes* THE REV HARRY HENDERSON, *who has a big McDonalds' bag full of teas and coffees and apple pies. He is smooth-skinned, smooth-voiced, short and dumpy, in his mid fifties, in a green tweed jacket and grey flannels.*)

HARRY: Harry's here.

LIONEL: Fine.

STREAKY: Good to see you, Harry.

HARRY: Delighted to be here. (*He starts distributing the contents of the big paper bag.*) Goodness, what a day!

STREAKY: Me too.

HARRY: Tea for you?

STREAKY: Thank you.

HARRY: And guess what I'm doing tonight. We're calling in the
diocesan exorcist.

STREAKY: Gosh. Lucky chap.

HARRY: I know. I'm terribly excited. I've never done one. I've
had to look up the service.

(LIONEL *carries on sorting his papers*. TONY *is watching, still*.)

STREAKY: I must say, I'm rather jealous.

HARRY: I know. It's a West Indian lady. With a lot of definite
nocturnal movement. She asked me to stay the night
actually. But I refused.

STREAKY: Very wise.

HARRY: I'm going to be shattered if something actually appears.
(*He smiles and hands* TONY *a cup of tea*.) Here you are,
Tony.

TONY: Oh, thank you.

HARRY: Are you all right?
(*He stops, puzzled by* TONY'*s manner*.)

TONY: No, I'm fine. It's silly.

LIONEL: (*Looking up*) Please go on, Tony.

TONY: No, it's just . . . no, it's nothing . . . before you both
arrived, Lionel and I were having a discussion.

HARRY: Oh, I see.
(TONY *is looking across at* LIONEL. HARRY *waits, confused by
the silence*.)
What about?

TONY: We were discussing how much we should be pushing
Christ at people, and how much they should be left to find
him for themselves.
(*There's a silence*. HARRY *nods*.)

HARRY: Uh-huh.

LIONEL: Yes, that was it.

STREAKY: Gosh, well, that's a curly one . . .

LIONEL: Yes, well, you might say.

TONY: No, I'm sorry, this is the wrong moment . . .

HARRY: There isn't any problem. That's what we're here for.
Surely we can talk about things?

(*He frowns, puzzled at* TONY's *unease. He looks round the three others.* TONY *nods.*)

LIONEL: Surely.

TONY: It's just . . . look, really, I've no wish to criticize. It happened. I burst in on Lionel at work. There was this woman. Frankly, I watched her. I think *she* was fairly surprised. She'd come in, off her own bat, with a problem. We just said a prayer and sent her away.

HARRY: Well?

TONY: Well nothing. It's fine. As far as it goes. It's just . . . the churches are empty.

(*He shrugs slightly. No one replies.* LIONEL *sits down, thoughtfully.*)

I don't know. I'm just asking if these two facts are linked.

(*There's a silence, no one wanting to jump in, waiting for* LIONEL, *who is impassive.*)

STREAKY: Got you.

TONY: Look, we work hard, for goodness' sake. We're at it all hours. Perhaps we work so hard we have no time to stop and see what's happening. The statistics are appalling. We feel we've had a good Sunday if between us we attract one per cent. One per cent of our whole catchment area. All right, I know this is terribly vulgar, numbers aren't everything – it's the quality of the experience and so on – but I would have said, 'Look madam, actually next Sunday we will perform an act of worship which it might do you some real good to attend.'

(*They frown at this, thoughtful.*)

STREAKY: Mmm, well, it's possible.

(TONY *waits, then getting no response bursts with frustration.*)

TONY: I want a full church. Is that so disgraceful? I want to see the whole community worshipping under one roof. I'm the junior member, this is my first parish, I've no right to bring this up. We can go about our business, we can look at our schedules, but really if in three years we don't fill the churches on Sunday, I'm sorry, then I think we'll have failed.

(*There's a silence.* STREAKY *looks across from his tea.*)

STREAKY: What do you say, Lionel?

LIONEL: Me? (*Frowns, coming out of a dream.*) Oh, I was thinking
. . . I saw Charlie Southwark.

STREAKY: Golly. How was he?

LIONEL: Unchanged.

STREAKY: Good scoff?

LIONEL: Fishcakes.

HARRY: His wife's a very good cook.

LIONEL: Yes, I know. He told me.

STREAKY: You missed out with fishcakes. I had grouse the only
time I went. I'd never had grouse. (*Chuckles happily.*) Isn't it
something? Being a bishop, eh?

TONY: What did he want?

LIONEL: Charlie? (*Looks at him a moment.*) That's why I
mentioned it. I was thinking, where have I had this feeling
before?

STREAKY: What, you mean with the bishop?

LIONEL: And with Tony. You give me the same feeling.
(*He now looks at* TONY *very directly.*)

TONY: What feeling?
(LIONEL *is very quiet, as if the others weren't there.*)

LIONEL: Forgive me. It's like I'm being pulled into line.
(HEATHER ESPY *comes in. She is in her early fifties, but has
adopted an older look. Skirt and cardigan, her hair prematurely
grey.*)

HEATHER: The paper man is here. You haven't paid the bill.

LIONEL: Oh Lord, I haven't had time to go to the bank.
(*They have all got up.*)
Does anyone have any money?

STREAKY: I've got some.

LIONEL: Thank you, Streaky.
(STREAKY *has got out his wallet.*)

HEATHER: And I need to go to the Asian shop.
(LIONEL *looks appealingly at* STREAKY, *who counts out some
more notes.*)

TONY: How are you, Mrs Espy?

HEATHER: Oh, I'm very well, thank you, Tony. (*Takes the
money.*) Lionel, you know it's Alex's concert?

LIONEL: Yes. Absolutely.

HEATHER: You won't let him down?

17

LIONEL: I may let him down. But I'm not yet admitting it.
(*She looks at him.*)
Please, I shall try. Thank you, darling.

HEATHER: I'll see you all later. Are you staying for supper?
(STREAKY *looks between them all.*)

STREAKY: We'll see.
(HEATHER *smiles and goes.* LIONEL *has already shifted his papers into piles, and begun distributing them.*)

LIONEL: Let's think. Now, where are we? A schedule for everyone. I've had to shift some visits for the sick.

HARRY: Thank you.

LIONEL: Streaky, if you could do a couple of extra home Communions, then I can do the hospital on Wednesday afternoon.

STREAKY: Yes, gladly.

HARRY: Look at this. He hasn't left me a single empty square! (*Shakes his head at the schedule.*) Will I ever get my nice parish in the country?

STREAKY: You'd hate it.

HARRY: I don't know.
(LIONEL *slaps down another load of paperwork on the table.*)

LIONEL: Bumf. (*More.*) Bumf. I must say, I sometimes think that if the Lord Jesus returned today, the Church of England would ask him to set out his ideas on a single sheet of A4.
(STREAKY *has got up and is now undoing his knapsack.*)

STREAKY: Oh listen, that reminds me, I called by Church House on the way. (*Piles pamphlets on to the table.*) A gross of *Mission in the City.* (*Holds up another.*) *The Art of Prayer in a Divided Society.* Look, it's called *Not on Your Knees.* Here's another. *Not Strangers but Pilgrims.* (*He is looking at the cover, and laughs.*) I haven't the slightest idea what that means. You can read it on ghostwatch.
(*He turns to* HARRY, *laughing.* HARRY *takes it.* LIONEL *is now assembling papers of different colours for committee meetings, which he begins to hand out.*)

TONY: Look, I'm sorry, are we going to talk about what I just said?

LIONEL: If you like.
(*He looks up from the table. He is very mild.*)

18

TONY: It does *matter*.

LIONEL: Yes. But this matters. (*Smiles, holding another batch of paper.*) In a way, I think, Tony, this matters more. (*Gets up and walks across to him, offering more paper, very quietly.*) Pink? And do you have green?

(TONY *takes them and goes to sit down, rather sulkily.*)

TONY: So what did you think of my criticisms?

LIONEL: What you saw was an exercise in pastoral duty. Everyone does it differently. In my view, that's fine. As long as you do it from the heart, in a way which is unforced and that suits you, then there's no problem. The problems start when you step out of character. That does no good at all. (*Smiles.*) I saw a black preacher – a woman – just the other day, stop at a bus queue. She couldn't resist it. There hadn't been a 2B for hours. And she just started telling them that Christ was their saviour. I admired her. That's her style. There's nothing wrong with it. Far from it, it's wonderful. (*Looks across to* TONY.) But if I did it, it would be wrong. (*He shrugs slightly, the matter closed, as* TONY *frowns, uncomprehending.*)

TONY: Yes, all right, but you can't just be complacent.

LIONEL: I'm not.

TONY: We're in a team, we must have something in common.

LIONEL: We do.

TONY: Well, what?

LIONEL: A desire to help people.

TONY: And?

LIONEL: A belief.

TONY: Yes. Are we making that clear?

(LIONEL *looks at him, as if there is no answer to this.*)
And in what?

LIONEL: In God everlasting. As I understand it. And in his Son, who came so that people might know God was close. And in the Holy Spirit. Who of the three always seems to me much the most mysterious. Much the shadiest, as you might say. (*He smiles, and* STREAKY *and* HARRY *smile too.*)

STREAKY: Yes.

(TONY *looks between them, bewildered by their shared humour.*)

TONY: But does anything else hold us together?

LIONEL: Of course. I'd have thought that was obvious.

TONY: Not to me.

(LIONEL *smiles again,* STREAKY *looking down as if he knew the answer.*)

LIONEL: Why, Tony, surely the fact that we're friends?

SCENE FIVE

The church. The REV TONY FERRIS *is on his knees, praying to God. He is fairly irate.*

TONY: You know I'm damned if I get this. I'm damned if I know what the hell's going on. Forgive my language. Lord, it's frightening. I can't believe I'm still the same man. I mean, when I was a student I was actually quite easygoing. I spent all my time at the Film Society and running the Campaign for Real Ale. But now I can actually feel my sense of humour departing. It's gone. Can you tell me, is anything *right* with the Church? I mean, is the big joke that having lived and died on the cross, Jesus would bequeath us – what? – total confusion, a host of good intentions, and an endlessly revolving cyclostyle machine? Is he really entrusting his Divine Mission to people like the Reverend Donald Bacon, universally known as *Streaky*?

I've got to pray for Lionel. I've got to. We are individuals. We have souls. Christ didn't come to sit on a committee. He didn't come to do social work. He came to preach repentance. And to offer everyone the chance of redemption. In their innermost being. God, please help Lionel to see this. Because otherwise I think things are going to get rough.

SCENE SIX

Harry's flat in Lambeth. It's warmly lit, in the evening, attractively decorated in a comfortable style. EWAN *is in his early twenties, in light jeans and a shirt, with no shoes on. He is reading a comic. On a table beside him, under a lamp, is a pile of comics.* HARRY *is standing immediately over the pile. He picks up a small passport-sized photo.* EWAN *is Scottish.*

HARRY: What's this?
EWAN: Oh, it's a photo. From one of those machines.
    (HARRY *puts it down.*)
HARRY: And you want me to find it? Is that why you leave it there?
EWAN: I don't know what you mean. (*Carries on reading his comic.*)
HARRY: Are you going out?
EWAN: No. Are you?
HARRY: How long are you staying for?
EWAN: I don't know. Till I've read a few books, I suppose.
    (HARRY *goes and sits down, takes out a pad of paper and a pen.*)
    Is that all right?
HARRY: Yes, of course. I've got to write my sermon.
EWAN: Make it good.
HARRY: Yes, I will.
    (HARRY *starts to write. Then* EWAN *looks up.*)
EWAN: It's no one. It's just a friend of mine. He gave me a lift. Down part of the motorway.
    (HARRY *goes on writing.*)
    What do you want? What do you want me to say? Give *me* the bloody photo.
HARRY: It's there.
EWAN: We were arsing about. (*Reaches for it and puts it in his pocket.*) I need a job.
HARRY: Yes, I know.
EWAN: I'm going to go back.
HARRY: Go back up to Glasgow? Yes, well, if you can't get work here, then you should.
    (*There's a pause. Then* EWAN *is suddenly bitter.*)
EWAN: All right, then, what? What do you want? I don't speak to anyone? You tell me, is that what you want?
HARRY: I don't want anything.
    (EWAN *looks down.*)

EWAN: I can get a job actually. I could get it, I'm sure. You know that theatre in a pub? In the Kennington Road?

HARRY: Ah, yes.

EWAN: I met a friend of the guy who runs it. He said you two were at Cambridge together.

HARRY: Yes, I know who you mean.

EWAN: Do you think . . .

(*He stops a moment.*)

HARRY: What?

EWAN: Just have a word with him? Say you know me? And how like I'm very good. Will you?

HARRY: Yes. (*Pauses, looking at him.*) I mean, if you like.

EWAN: You don't want to?

HARRY: I'll do it.

EWAN: Is even that too much?

(*There's a pause.* EWAN *looks away.*)

Do you know what I hate?

HARRY: No, I don't.

EWAN: I hate the bloody church.

HARRY: Ah yes.

EWAN: They're a bunch of hypocrites. I thought the whole deal was meant to be about love.

HARRY: So it is.

EWAN: And you can't go to a friend and say, there's this young man, please will you give him a job? What a bunch of bloody hypocrites!

HARRY: Yes. Yes, you said.

(HARRY *just looks at him.* EWAN *suddenly shouts*)

EWAN: I need a job.

HARRY: I know. We will get you one.

EWAN: But not too near you, is that what you mean?

(*There's a pause.* HARRY *puts his pad aside. Quietly.*)

HARRY: I've always told you. It's very simple. There are people in the parish who don't like the idea.

EWAN: And there are so bloody few of them, you can't afford to lose one.

HARRY: It isn't like that.

EWAN: They've got you, Harry. And they know it. You have no choice. They can be as vindictive and nasty as they want to

22

be. And you have to put up with it. You have to dance to their stupid tune.

HARRY: It isn't true. It's simply . . . (*Pauses, to make his thoughts clear.*) I am the vessel. I am only the channel through which God's love can pass. That makes me, as a person, totally irrelevant. As a person, nobody should even be conscious I'm there. If I do something which is in any sense worrying . . . if I upset my communicants in any way, then the focus is moved. From the Lord Jesus. On to his minister. And that is not where the focus belongs.

(EWAN *turns away.* HARRY *smiles.*)

Yes. It doesn't matter whether I wish things might be different . . .

EWAN: It's hypocritical.

HARRY: I may disapprove their intolerance. However. It's as if I chose to walk down the street in a bright red suit, blowing bubbles out of my ears. It would distract attention. It would alter the agenda. And that is something for which God would not forgive me. And rightly.

(EWAN *shakes his head, in pain.*)

EWAN: Why don't you fight? Why don't you fight for me? That's all I want. To be loved enough so that someone will fight for me. So that I can start to exist.

HARRY: I would like to fight. But it's not possible.

(*It is suddenly very quiet.* HARRY *has tears in his eyes.*)

Ewan, don't give up on me. Without you, I'm chaff.

(*There is another silence. Then* EWAN *gets up from his chair, moved and angry.*)

EWAN: Why do you do this? It's not fair. What is it? You always upset me so much. I come down to London with such high hopes. There's never any comfort. I want some comfort, you know.

HARRY: Yes.

EWAN: I'm an actor. Everyone looks to me to say, 'You're not an actor, you're a speck of dirt. You're dirt. If you're an actor, then act.' (*Turns to* HARRY, *replying*) 'I can't act. I can't get a job.'

(HARRY *looks down.*)

You sit there.

23

HARRY: I do.

EWAN: And you never come back at me. Why do you think I'm fart-arsing about on the motorway? Why do you think I leave photos around? (*He looks at him.*) I just need a *gesture*. (HARRY *smiles*.)

HARRY: I'm a priest. I have to soak up my punishment.

EWAN: I come here because no one else loves me. And yet I always leave here confused.

HARRY: Yes.

(EWAN *turns away*.)

EWAN: Let's go for a drink. Not on the other side of London. Right here. The bar down the road.

(*He turns, catching the momentary hesitation in* HARRY's *eyes*.)

All right, forget it.

(*Before* HARRY *can protest,* EWAN *shouts*.)

Forget it. All right? (*Goes back to his chair angrily, and begins putting his shoes on.*) Read me your sermon. Why not? Read it. I want to know. What you will say. Next Sunday. I'll be in Glasgow. I'm going back. I've had it.

(HARRY *looks at him, not moving*.)

If I could be with you . . . if I were with you . . . come on, tell me . . . what would I hear you say?

SCENE SEVEN

The glistening tarmac of a South London street in the rain at night. The door of a council house, with an open area, sodium lit in front of it. TONY *knocks on the door, then waits. Then* STELLA *appears. She is in carpet slippers and a nightgown. She is wearing dark glasses. One side of her face is bandaged. The minute she sees who it is, she looks back into the house.*

TONY: Hello. Good evening.

STELLA: What's this?

TONY: I'm sorry to bother you. I'm the Rev Tony Ferris.

STELLA: What d'you mean?

TONY: What do I *mean*? Don't you remember? We met very briefly. Do you remember? I'm the curate at St Matthew's.

24

(STELLA *looks at him a moment.*)

Look, I just felt there should be some follow-up. This would be much easier if we could do it indoors.

(STELLA *leads him away from the door, moving across the open area.*)

STELLA: I don' wanna talk to you. I talked to the vicar.

TONY: I heard about your accident.

(*Before she can speak he interrupts.*)

Please, Mrs Marr. I visited the shop.

STELLA: Why? What for? Who asked you?

TONY: They gave me your address. That's why I'm here. I know you've not been in to work.

STELLA: I can't go to work.

TONY: No, I see that.

STELLA: I told 'em at the hospital.

TONY: What happened?

STELLA: Nothin'. I spilt a saucepan.

TONY: Yes? How did you spill it?

STELLA: Off the stove.

TONY: What was in it?

STELLA: Water.

TONY: How did you spill it?

STELLA: Careless.

TONY: Yes, I mean, how is that physically possible?

(*There is a pause.*)

Stella, is your husband in there? (*Looks at her a moment.*) Come on, we both know what's going on. You need my help. Where is he? Don't be stupid. Do you take me for a fool? I've come to help you.

STELLA: I'm not bein' stupid. What the hell's goin' on? What the hell business is it of yours?

(*He moves in towards her.*)

TONY: Stella, you're very scared.

STELLA: No, I'm not.

TONY: You're terrified.

STELLA: I'm not scared. I din' come to you. I come to the other man. I wouldn'a' come if I'd known you'd come back. (*Looks at him fiercely.*) All I want is to try and get over it. You say you want to help. Well you can. I tell you

25

how you help. You help me by staying away.

(TONY *moves towards her again.*)

TONY: Can I tell you something? Jesus has your interests at heart. Yes, he does. But he can't help you – I tell you this from my own experience – he can't help you until you admit your own problems to yourself . . .

(*She turns and goes back towards the house. He pursues her.*) Oh yes, and if that means my standing here – yes! – *standing* here outside this house until I find your husband, until I get him to face what he's done, then OK. I can wait here for days. I am actually sick of it. Letting everything go by. If he won't admit it, I'll go to the police. (*Suddenly gestures to his dog collar.*) What, he thinks I can't do anything because this is round my neck?

(*She turns.*)

STELLA: I got to go.

(*He moves towards her.*)

TONY: I shall be here. Don't be frightened. We're going to protect you.

STELLA: I think I better go in.

SCENE EIGHT

The Espy's kitchen. HEATHER *comes in, followed by* FRANCES, *who is shaking out a wet umbrella. She also has a raincoat on. The kitchen has been largely appropriated for gardening: the table is covered with flowerpots and cuttings. It's evening.*

HEATHER: You're welcome, Miss Parnell. I'm afraid it'll be only instant.

FRANCES: That's fine.

HEATHER: We don't have real. It was clever of you to carry an umbrella.

FRANCES: Oh . . . I actually . . . I always do.

HEATHER: The wise virgin.

FRANCES: Yes, well. In a way.

(HEATHER *takes her coat and umbrella from her.*)

What a nice house.

26

HEATHER: Lionel's on his rounds. He gives Communion to the house-bound on Tuesdays. Then he's chairman of the local school.

FRANCES: Oh yes?

HEATHER: Yes. And a housing charity. Also ex-prisoners. There's a discussion group. And the mentally ill. They believe now in something called care in the community. That means closing down the hospitals and letting them wander the streets. So Lionel does a group. That's also Tuesdays.

FRANCES: I wonder you see him at all.

HEATHER: Well, I don't.

(FRANCES *frowns, puzzled by the mildness of* HEATHER's *manner*.)

FRANCES: And you have children?

HEATHER: Alex is studying the clarinet. Lucy's in London.

FRANCES: Isn't this London?

HEATHER: Oh yes. (*Nods, vaguely.*) Somewhere else in London, I mean.

(FRANCES *nods at the piano.*)

FRANCES: Who plays the piano?

HEATHER: Oh, I did. Not any longer. Lionel can't think when I play. So I stopped.

FRANCES: So what do you do instead?

HEATHER: Well, there's the garden.

FRANCES: I'm friends with Tony.

HEATHER: Tony?

FRANCES: Your husband's curate.

HEATHER: Ah yes. Tony. (*Frowns, as if thinking about it.*) Is he a nice man?

(*But before* FRANCES *can answer,* LIONEL *appears, soaking wet, his head drenched and his jacket dripping.*)

LIONEL: Ah, there you are. We spoke on the telephone.

FRANCES: Yes.

LIONEL: I should have learnt by now. I had no umbrella.

HEATHER: The foolish virgin.

LIONEL: What did you say?

(HEATHER *automatically takes his soaking jacket.*)

HEATHER: I'll get you a towel.

27

(HEATHER *goes out. Lionel's shirt is wet under his jacket.*)

LIONEL: We have met.

FRANCES: Yes. Briefly.

LIONEL: I remember, aren't you an East Anglian Parnell?

(FRANCES *smiles.*)

You also seemed to be best friends with Tony.

FRANCES: That's right. I was. I knew him quite well. His parents were killed. A while back.

LIONEL: Yes, I knew that.

FRANCES: I helped him through it. But he tended to bury me away in the background.

LIONEL: Really?

FRANCES: Yes. I was sort of unofficial.

(*He looks straight at her for the first time.*)

LIONEL: Golly. I can't think why.

(HEATHER *appears with a tray on which there is coffee and milk and sugar, and some macaroons. She also has a towel over her arm.*)

Oh, please let me help, I'll take that.

HEATHER: Can you manage with the pouring?

LIONEL: Yes.

HEATHER: The milk is in there.

LIONEL: Thank you.

(*They have cleared space on the table to set it down.*)

Bless you, Heather.

HEATHER: Lionel, I'll be in the back.

(*She goes out again.* LIONEL *has started drying his hair with the towel.* FRANCES *has not moved.*)

FRANCES: Tony hid me away because . . . well you know Tony.

LIONEL: Yes.

FRANCES: Have you seen him lately? I think he's changed. He's changed a good deal. It's why I've come to see you. (*Pauses a moment.*) I don't want him making a fool of himself.

(LIONEL *frowns, not understanding.*)

LIONEL: In what way?

FRANCES: Look, I'll tell you . . . it just happens I went home at the weekend. My parents are in Norfolk. You know I'm from this big church-going family.

LIONEL: Of course. The Parnells.

FRANCES: The house was full of bishops. Nothing unusual in that.

LIONEL: Which bishops?

FRANCES: Manchester. Chester. Exeter. And Charlie Southwark.

LIONEL: Mmm. That doesn't sound good.

(*He grimaces. She smiles.*)

FRANCES: My uncle had got them together because he's chairman of the agency. The church had got hold of this idea that it wants to start advertising. He's offering our services free. But then at dinner the Bishops rolled up their sleeves. Chester said if they were running any other kind of business, they could make rational decisions. (*Slows down.*) And that's when Southwark began to talk about you.

(LIONEL *looks at her, recognizing the seriousness of her tone.*)

LIONEL: What did he say?

FRANCES: He was complaining about how you run your parish. He said all your old crowd didn't know where they were. And there was no new crowd. He then said . . . (*Hesitates, nervous.*)

LIONEL: Go on.

FRANCES: He'd spoken to you. Things were no better. He said it was kind of a test case. He'd decided you'd have to go.

(*There is a pause. She waits for his reaction. But after a while, he is quiet.*)

LIONEL: Well, well.

FRANCES: Look, the point is, I also saw Tony.

(*There's a pause.*)

He hit a man. Did you know this?

LIONEL: No.

FRANCES: Late one night. Afterwards he got very drunk. And came round to my place. Now he's given up drink. He says, for ever.

LIONEL: What happened?

FRANCES: I think he was trying to help a parishioner. He was convinced this man had thrown hot water in his wife's face. He'd been lying in wait for him. There was some sort of argument. Then he actually did swing a punch.

LIONEL: Is he all right?

(FRANCES *leans forward*.)

FRANCES: He's spinning like a top, Mr Espy.

LIONEL: Lionel.

FRANCES: He came round straight afterwards. He was frightening. He went round my flat shouting 'Waffle! Waffle!' at the top of his voice all the time. He said 'What are we offering? What are we actually offering?'

(LIONEL *frowns*.)

LIONEL: What did he do then?

FRANCES: Oh, you know. I couldn't get rid of him. He was raving. I went to bed. When I woke up, I went into the sitting room. He was still sitting at the desk. He just turned and looked at me. He said nothing. He then got up and walked out of the room. (*Looks down, hurt now*.) I thought at first the problem was exhaustion. He's thrown himself at the job. He's incredibly naïve. He wants to get hold of people and solve them.

LIONEL: It's a common failing. When you first start. (*Smiles*.) You go in too hard. Usually with a lot of talk about Jesus. Always a danger sign in my experience. I'll have a word with him.

FRANCES: Yes. I think you should.

LIONEL: I will.

FRANCES: And quickly. Tony's going to go to the current Synod. He's been asked by the Bishop.

(LIONEL *looks at her*.)

Yes, exactly. That's why I came. Lionel, Southwark is assembling a case against you. And now he's going to ask Tony's help.

(LIONEL *looks at her a moment. It is so still it is as if they are both holding their breath*.)

LIONEL: Are you two still together?

(*She doesn't answer*.)

But you're still in love with him?

(*She looks down*.)

It still hurts.

FRANCES: I'm fearful he'll do something he later regrets.

(LIONEL *looks at her a moment, thoughtfully*.)

30

LIONEL: Do you know this area?

FRANCES: Yes.

LIONEL: It can be pretty punishing. I don't think anyone fr⌐
the outside quite understands what the job is. Mostly it's
just listening to the anger. One reason or another. Lately
it's the change in the DSS rules. If you're young, setting up
home, you can no longer get a loan for a stove, unless you
can prove you'll be able to pay the money back. I've had
three couples in the last week. They need somewhere to go
to express their frustration. They're drawn to a priest.
They're furious. At their lives. At the system. At where
they find themselves. (*Smiles.*) And they come to the vicar
because he's the one man who can never hit back.

(FRANCES *is restless, not understanding.*)

FRANCES: Yes, I'm sure but I mean . . . you can fight in *this*
case?

(*He looks at her a moment, as if in a dream.*)

LIONEL: I'm sorry?

FRANCES: You do still have the will? Don't you? (*Frowns.*)
You're not saying you'll just sit there and let them dislodge
you?

LIONEL: Oh, good Lord, no I wouldn't do that.

(FRANCES *looks at him, for the first time a little bit fazed by his
manner.*)

FRANCES: I mean, I know, look it's none of my business . . .

LIONEL: Please.

FRANCES: The one thing I do understand: the Church's system
is founded on freehold.

LIONEL: Yes, absolutely.

FRANCES: Once a vicar's there, he can stay for as long as he
likes.

LIONEL: That's right. It's a job for life. It's sort of wonderful.

FRANCES: But that's what's so crazy. Southwark says you once
had freehold here.

LIONEL: Ah, so I did.

FRANCES: But you gave it up. For a five-year contract. Which
is coming to an end.

LIONEL: Well, I mean, technically yes.

FRANCES: Technically?

(LIONEL *leans forward, anxious to explain.*)

LIONEL: Look, obviously, we all decided, here in this area, it was put to us and we agreed, it was our decision, we wanted a team. And with a team, it doesn't make sense to cling on to freehold. Because what happens if – in everyone else's eyes – one team member isn't pulling his weight? It isn't fair to the others. So, as a group, we decided, just in case we didn't get on, we'd go for a formula which put the interests of the team first. (*Smiles contentedly.*) And the Bishop, to be fair, was terribly keen on it.

FRANCES: Yes, well, he would be, wouldn't he?

LIONEL: Oh, really, come on. This isn't party politics. People's minds just don't work like that.

(FRANCES *suddenly raises her voice, exasperated.*)

FRANCES: I was at the dinner. Southwark's out to get you.

LIONEL: Frances, I am not an absolute fool.

(FRANCES *blushes, shocked by her outburst.*)

FRANCES: No, really, of course, I didn't mean that.

LIONEL: I'm not an idiot, I could see there might be a difficulty there. So I went to my suffragan Bishop.

FRANCES: Is that Kingston?

LIONEL: That's right. (*Nods.*) I said, 'Look, we love our new system, marvellous, much more progressive and so on, but between you and me, I know this is embarrassing, it won't be used, will it, as a way of throwing chaps overboard?' (*Sits back.*) And it was fine.

FRANCES: How?

LIONEL: He gave me a promise. There's no problem. Gilbert gave me his word. (*Blows on his hand, as if to signal the problem being blown away.*)

So there it is. Shadow-boxing.

(FRANCES *frowns.*)

FRANCES: Lionel, can't Kingston be overruled?

LIONEL: Overruled? How?

FRANCES: Kingston's the deputy. He works under Southwark. Southwark's the boss. So what happens if Southwark just says no? 'Doesn't matter what my junior said. Forget it.'

LIONEL: You can't overrule a promise. How can you? (*Shakes*

his head as if this were self-evidently absurd.) It was freely
given. It was in good faith. I mean, now I sound
patronizing, which I always hate. But you don't
understand the church. It has its weak moments. But this
was a promise. And that's the end of it.
(*He smiles.* FRANCES *looks at him, worried.*)

FRANCES: Perhaps at least you should have that word with
Tony.

LIONEL: Certainly. Good Lord, yes. Now where's my little
diary? (*Takes it from his trouser pocket.*) Probably not this
week.

FRANCES: Lionel.

LIONEL: What?

FRANCES: Do it this week.

LIONEL: All right. I'm sorry. Yes. (*Smiles, then looks up.*) Tony
was fortunate. People talk to us all the time. We don't
have anyone we can talk to.

FRANCES: No.
(*There's a pause.*)

LIONEL: Now I know Tony's crazy. To have given you up.
(*She smiles and gets up to get her coat.*)

FRANCES: How do you know he did?

LIONEL: Sadly . . .

FRANCES: Perhaps I gave him up.

LIONEL: I wish it were true. But it's always the wrong way. He
doesn't deserve you. (*Looks away.*) I'm sorry. That was
unchristian.

FRANCES: Extremely.

LIONEL: No, it wasn't fair.

FRANCES: No. But it was human.
(*She has her coat and umbrella. He looks at her, still not up
from the table.*)
I'd say it was the most reassuring thing I heard. (*Moves
towards the door.*) Call me if you need help.

LIONEL: I give help. I don't need it.

FRANCES: Not yet.

The church. FRANCES *walks in, smiling. She looks round like one who has been away a long time.*

FRANCES: This is stupid. May I say I don't even believe in you? Mind you, nor does anyone I know. Except my family. Who don't count. And Tony. And Lionel, in his own way. In other words you're fielding a very weak team. Whereas my lot – the non-believers – you'd have to say we're looking pretty sharp.

I didn't enjoy my visit with the vicar. Why did they choose Lionel? It could have been anyone. Is Lionel that much worse than all the rest?

Or is he just unlucky? There isn't any justice, that's clear. You're not a moral God. Your style is more 'What a sweet baby! Wham! Give it cancer!' Just as soon as anyone begins to get happy, you put them in a plane crash, and pfft! The whole thing's a joke.

If there were justice then I'd believe in you. I like the idea of justice better than God. Because God is arbitrary.

As everyone knows. Except Lionel. And he will very shortly find out.

SCENE TEN

A high bar, in the modern style. At the bar, sideways on, on a high stool, is TOMMY ADAIR, *in his mid-fifties. He is fat, androgynous, oddly like a woman in drag, with wavy hair. He is smoking a cigarette, and has a sweet drink.* EWAN *has his back to us, leaning on the bar, drinking a half of lager.*

TOMMY: Well, this is nice.

(EWAN *does not turn.*)

This is nice.

EWAN: I'm sorry?

(*He turns, realizing it's him being spoken to.*)

TOMMY: Aren't you a friend of a friend?

EWAN: Am I really?

TOMMY: I've got a lot of friends. What do you do on Sunday?

EWAN: Sunday?

TOMMY: Yes.

(EWAN *is mystified*.)

EWAN: What do *you* do?

TOMMY: Oh, I eat roast beef and make love to my wife. (*Smiles.*) I work for a well-known British institution.

EWAN: Oh aye.

TOMMY: Which comes wrapped in the Union Jack. So do I. So does my wife. With a bit of luck round five o'clock she sings 'Land of Hope and Glory'.

EWAN: I reckon you're a journalist.

TOMMY: Yes. How did you guess?

(EWAN *looks at him mistrustfully*.)

EWAN: Oh, I'm quick that way.

TOMMY: Yes, I gather.

(*There's a pause.*)

EWAN: What does that mean?

(TOMMY *picks up his drink*.)

TOMMY: I gather it's all been ruined by AIDS. On our paper we take a patriotic interest in deviant sex.

EWAN: Is that what you call it?

TOMMY: I hear it's got very boring. You can't actually *do* anything, is that right? Or are there ways round it?

(EWAN *just looks at him*.)

EWAN: How would I know?

TOMMY: That's what they tell me. They say you just lie there. And then you have to attend to yourself.

(EWAN *makes to go*.)

EWAN: I have to go.

TOMMY: Are you an actor? You look like an actor.

EWAN: Who told you that?

TOMMY: I bet you're really good. Aren't you? You look as if you could be really good.

(EWAN *hovers a moment, indecisive*.)

The readers I'm afraid are literal-minded. They need very long descriptions. In very short words. They don't look for a new way of putting it. As we know, it can only be put in so many ways.

(He smiles. EWAN *makes to go again.)*

EWAN: Right, thank you. I think I understand you.

TOMMY: The Church does not eat roast beef with its wife.

*(*EWAN *is still.)*

Ewan, I am talking about sums of money so large that they would fund the Press Council for a year. But we must have specifics.

EWAN: I'm away.

TOMMY: Please take my card.

(He reaches out with it. EWAN *moves over and takes it. Then puts it in his own half-finished drink.)*

EWAN: You'll never get me, you know? You won't get anyone. I'll tell you why. Because what people still have . . . which is theirs . . . which belongs to them . . . which is precious . . . is what happens in private.

*(*TOMMY *does not react.)*

That's right. And that's why you want it. That's why you want to slime all over it. Because it *is* private. And in private, there's still some decency.

*(*TOMMY *smiles.)*

TOMMY: You've got a sweet smile. They said you had.

*(*EWAN *goes.)*

I'll be in touch.

SCENE ELEVEN

Church House. The empty chamber of the Synod. Early morning. A golden roof with a circular legend, in gold, HOLY IS THE TRUE LIGHT AND PASSING WONDERFUL TO THEM THAT ENDURED IN THE HEAT OF THE CONFLICT: FROM CHRIST THEY INHERIT A HOME OF UNFADING SPLENDOUR WHEREIN THEY REJOICE WITH GLADNESS EVERMORE. *From opposite sides appear* 'STREAKY' BACON, *together with* HARRY HENDERSON, *and from the other, in full purple, the* BISHOP OF KINGSTON, GILBERT HEFFERNAN. *He is young for a bishop, only in his forties, and with lean jaw, and slim, athletic build.*

KINGSTON: Streaky.

36

STREAKY: Bishop. It's good of you to see us.

KINGSTON: I always forget you're a member of Synod. I don't know why.

STREAKY: I was voted in recently. Someone put me up for a lark. In a by-election. On a 'Mission not Maintenance' ticket.

KINGSTON: You're not 'Church in Danger'?

STREAKY: Well, actually not.

KINGSTON: Thank goodness for that.

(*They both smile at this.*)

STREAKY: I did flirt for a while with 'Prayer Book Preservation'.

KINGSTON: That's an excellent ticket.

STREAKY: You do know Harry?

KINGSTON: Of course.

HARRY: Gilbert.

(*They shake hands.*)

STREAKY: This is Harry's first visit.

KINGSTON: Well, you've chosen a good one. Freemasonry. It'll be lively.

HARRY: I hope so.

KINGSTON: Feelings run high.

(*There's a moment's pause.*)

We go back a long way. I was thinking it was Harry who first recommended me for *Thought for the Day*.

HARRY: Yes, it's true. (*Smiles nervously, hating this.*) I was at school with the producer.

KINGSTON: I haven't heard you lately.

HARRY: I'm afraid not. (*Looks down.*) That producer moved on, you know how it is.

KINGSTON: Yes. For some reason – I can't think why – they actually give me every other Friday.

HARRY: Yes. I've heard you.

KINGSTON: It's quite a burden, of course. The responsibility. For so many people it's their only contact with religion. Every time I do it, I say to myself, 'Think, Gilbert, think: yes, all right, jokes, fine, little stories, but finally are you stuffing enough into this slot?'

STREAKY: Yes.

(*He takes a sidelong glance at* HARRY, *who looks ironically back*.) Yes, well, I sense that.

KINGSTON: In the studio there's a round table. Harry will know this. I think it's psychologically crucial, don't you? I always think, 'Right, I'm on one side and there on the other is Mrs Smith, getting breakfast, all the little Smiths, maybe Mr Smith's driving in to work, and just for a moment I say, "Hold on, Mrs Smith, a word in your ear."' (*Looks straight at* STREAKY.) And that has its place.

STREAKY: I'm sure she's very grateful.

KINGSTON: I get hundreds of letters.

(STREAKY *takes a quick glance at* HARRY.)

STREAKY: You could say . . . in a way . . . Harry sort of set you on your career.

KINGSTON: Yes. (*Pauses, not liking the turn in the conversation*.) On part of my career.

STREAKY: Yes.

KINGSTON: One small part of it. Broadcasting is only one aspect of what I do.

STREAKY: Quite.

HARRY: (*Quietly*) I wouldn't claim credit.

(*The atmosphere has cooled. But* HARRY *looks modest and genuine*.)

KINGSTON: And what exactly did you want to ask?

(STREAKY *and* HARRY *look to one another*.)

HARRY: Well . . .

STREAKY: No, you say . . .

HARRY: It's about Lionel.

KINGSTON: Lionel, bless him.

HARRY: Yes. He's been very worried.

KINGSTON: He wouldn't be Lionel unless he were worried.

HARRY: No. There's a rumour his contract won't be renewed.

(*There's a second's pause*.)

KINGSTON: Really? Well, if there is, I haven't heard it.

HARRY: A couple of years ago you gave him an assurance. On this very subject.

KINGSTON: Did I?

HARRY: Yes, apparently.

(*A short pause*.)

STREAKY: Lionel says you did. Didn't you?

KINGSTON: Well if Lionel said it, then I must have done.

HARRY: Will you testify you did?

KINGSTON: 'Testify'! What language! Are we at that stage? What is the source of this rumour?

HARRY: Someone heard Charlie.

KINGSTON: I see.

HARRY: Being quite vehement.

KINGSTON: In what forum?

STREAKY: At dinner.

(*A slight pause.*)

KINGSTON: So isn't it best you go directly to him?

STREAKY: Yes. We just needed to check.

KINGSTON: Check?

STREAKY: That your memory was holding up. That you'd be solid, so to speak. In your recollection. Before things got out of hand.

(KINGSTON *nods.*)

KINGSTON: Yes, I agree. I see that. The last thing we want is an issue.

STREAKY: Quite.

KINGSTON: I would say the heart of my job was preventing problems turning into issues.

HARRY: It's in nobody's interest.

KINGSTON: No. (*He smiles.*) That's the joy, you know, of committees. On any given subject, a committee may commission a report. The bishops may deliberate. In the goodness of time, the Synod may confer.

(STREAKY *looks ironically at* HARRY *behind* SOUTHWARK's *back.*)

There are so many questions when it comes to the crunch. But I have discovered, in the span of my ministry, that avoiding the crunch is what the whole thing's about.

HARRY: Indeed, yes that's true, I can see why you feel that . . .

KINGSTON: Yes.

HARRY: It's very ticklish. We know that Southwark would like Lionel to go. And Southwark, no doubt, believes he's well within his rights. But of course he's wrong. Because he doesn't know about your promise. Does he?

39

(HARRY *looks at* KINGSTON *who does not answer*.)

And it's really a question of when he finds out.

KINGSTON: Ah yes. (*Pauses*.) Yes, I can see that.

HARRY: And plainly, it's also important everyone's memories match. Say, for instance, you didn't recollect your meeting quite the way Lionel did . . . that would be very confusing all round.

(KINGSTON *looks thoughtfully at* HARRY.)

KINGSTON: Is Lionel here?

HARRY: No. We . . .

STREAKY: Perhaps it was wrong of us. We decided we should take matters in hand. On Lionel's behalf.

KINGSTON: I see.

STREAKY: Lionel has a combustible curate. Who is developing a rather evangelical tilt.

KINGSTON: Oh dear.

STREAKY: Yes. He's young. And from all the best motives. But it presents another problem as well. It's a touch ominous. This young man is quite disenchanted. And Southwark has asked him to dinner tonight.

(KINGSTON *looks at* STREAKY.)

KINGSTON: Yes, I must say.

STREAKY: That's where Lionel is. We told him to talk to this curate first. While we came here. And dealt with the other end.

(KINGSTON *shifts a moment*.)

KINGSTON: Yes. I'm just piecing this together. It does seem like very deep water. I'm not sure I should really intervene.

(HARRY *speaks with silky quiet*.)

HARRY: Mention the other thing.

STREAKY: Oh yes, I'm afraid there's one other factor, which could be quite ugly . . .

KINGSTON: (*Keeping calm*) Yes?

STREAKY: As you know, Lionel's church is just two miles from Westminster. There's a very nice Georgian terrace where MPs live because it's cheaper than Chelsea. One of these is a minister. He's Number Two at Transport. He hears Lionel's sermons. He's heard them for years. They tend to harp a bit on certain themes. The divided nation. The failings of materialism. The importance of devoting our lives to the poor. (*Pauses a second to see how this is going.*) He's a Tory minister who sits through it every Sunday. Imagine.

(KINGSTON *looks at him unkindly.*)

KINGSTON: Yes, I'm not sure you'll find this a very fruitful line of research.

(*Both* HARRY *and* STREAKY *leap in at once, animated.*)

STREAKY: I mean, come on . . .

HARRY: Well, what other reason . . .

STREAKY: Gilbert!

(KINGSTON *turns, raising his voice.*)

KINGSTON: No! Absolutely not!

HARRY: We're looking for a *motive* . . . .

STREAKY: Everyone *knows.*

HARRY: The minister is on the ecclesiastical committee of the House of Commons. You're not telling me he hasn't had a word with Southwark.

STREAKY: They play squash together!

(KINGSTON *shakes his head.*)

KINGSTON: This is really not something you should try to pursue.

HARRY: No?

KINGSTON: Under any circumstances. I couldn't help you. It's sheer innuendo. Southwark would go through the roof. And rightly. It's like a nail-bomb. You touch that subject, it goes off – are you crazy? – in every direction. (*Turns, confident.*) I can tell you right now, Arch would be furious. He's had it. We've all had it. And how on earth do you think you could prove such a thing?

(*He turns away a moment.* HARRY *smiles at* STREAKY, *pleased with this response.*)

Do you have any idea? Of what hell it is? Holding this bundle together? Oh, I'm sure from the parishes it all looks a big joke. That's because you're not actually involved. If you just stop and think for a moment . . . of what Arch actually has to do, every day . . . the tensions are impossible. Ever since we failed to confer on the

41

Falklands expedition, the theological status of a holy war.
Church and State are held together by a single thread.
(*Suddenly shouts, all his frustration coming out.*) It's not even
a thread! It's dental floss! (*Turns away, muttering now.*)
And you want to start making unfounded allegations.
(HARRY *is very quiet.*)

HARRY: Well, yes, that's exactly why we mentioned it. As
something none of us would wish to bring out.

KINGSTON: I'm very glad to hear it.

HARRY: We won't bring it out, will we Streaky?

STREAKY: Certainly not, old boy.

HARRY: Unless we have to.

KINGSTON: Have to?

HARRY: I mean . . .
(*He pauses, smiling seraphically.* STREAKY *watches in
admiration.*)
If after searching inside ourselves, we discovered a moral
obligation.
(KINGSTON *looks at him, unable to fathom the mildness of his
manner.*)
I mean, surely this is the very point you were making
earlier, Gilbert? You were very eloquent.

KINGSTON: I'm sorry?

HARRY: About the Church's role. Being to smooth paths.
(*There's a pause.*)

KINGSTON: Quite.

HARRY: Sort things out in private.

KINGSTON: Exactly.

HARRY: Avoid the dangers of polarization. With all the distress
open differences cause. Streaky and I both agree with you.
(*Smiles slightly.*) Good Christian practice means avoiding
the crunch.
(KINGSTON *looks at him a moment. He is imperturbable.*)

KINGSTON: Perhaps we should ask the real Christian question.
(*Pauses, suddenly sincere.*) Is he a good priest?
(*There is a moment.* HARRY *and* STREAKY *look to one
another to answer.*)

STREAKY: Harry's known him longer.

HARRY: How can you say?

(*There's a pause.*)
Lionel is patient and sincere.

KINGSTON: Is he a man of faith?

(HARRY *looks down.*)

HARRY: He's a man of conscience.

KINGSTON: What, and you think that's enough?

(*There's a silence.* KINGSTON *moves away. A second or two passes, then a bell begins to toll distantly*.)

All right, I'll help you look into it.

STREAKY: Thank you, Gilbert.

KINGSTON: Southwark won't like it. We're miles apart on women.

(STREAKY *and* HARRY *look confused by this.*)

STREAKY: What?

KINGSTON: Their ordination, I mean.

STREAKY: (*Smiles.*) Oh, I see.

(KINGSTON *turns, about to go.*)

KINGSTON: What I'm saying is, if I intervene, it may be counter-productive. But if you wish it.

HARRY: We'll take that chance.

(*The doors throughout the hall are thrown open. Clergy and laity flock in to take their places. Men in legal wigs and gowns assemble at the central table, as the hall fills.*)

KINGSTON: Well, here we go. A vigorous morning's debating. Rapier and bludgeon. Absolutely no holds barred. All opinions respected. And at the end, a view acceptable to everyone. Lord, guide our thoughts.

(*A bell is rung loudly. A* WOMAN *is heard offstage.*)

WOMAN: The Synod is in session. Let us pray.

(*At once there is silence. As the prayer in the hall continues, the lights go down until there is darkness.*)

ALL: Our Father,
Which art in heaven,
Hallowed be thy name.
Thy kingdom come,
Thy will be done,
On Earth as it is in Heaven.
Give us this day our daily bread,
And forgive us our trespasses,

As we forgive them that trespass against us,
And lead us not into temptation,
But deliver us from evil,
For thine is the kingdom, the power and the glory,
For ever and ever.
Amen.

SCENE TWELVE

The church. The lights have gone down through the prayers. At the end there is total darkness but for two candles in front of TONY's *kneeling figure. Behind him,* LIONEL *stands, unnoticed. On* TONY's *face, a look of intense concentration. The organ plays, subliminally.*

LIONEL: Tony.

> (TONY *doesn't hear.*)
> Tony.
> (*He hears but, transfixed, doesn't turn.*)

TONY: It's you, Lionel.

LIONEL: You look like a ghost.

> (TONY *turns and stares at him.*)
> I came in. I wanted . . . to ask you to dinner.

TONY: Dinner? That's very kind. But I can't. I've got . . . another invitation.

LIONEL: Really?

TONY: In town.

LIONEL: Oh yes?

TONY: I'm going to see . . .

> (*He stops. There is a very long pause.* LIONEL *is quite still. Then*) . . . someone else.
> (LIONEL *smiles:*)

LIONEL: Well, then, some other time.

TONY: Some other time, yes. (*Stares at him a moment.*) Well, I must be going, or else I'll be late. Good to see you, Lionel. (*Gets up from his knees.*) I'll see you soon.

> (*He begins to walk from the church. Then, towards the door, he accelerates and runs out.*
> LIONEL *alone. Steps forward and looks up to heaven.*)

44

LIONEL: What can you do, Lord? You tell me. You show me
the way. Go on. You explain why all this hurt has to
come. Tell me. You understand everything. (*Steps back.*)
Why do the good always fight among themselves?

ACT TWO

SCENE ONE

Savoy Hotel. The doors to the main dining-room. TONY *is coming through the lobby, heading hesitantly in unfamiliar surroundings. As he reaches the dining-room doors,* HARRY *steps out from a hiding place.*

HARRY: Tony.

TONY: Harry. What the dickens . . .
> (*At once the* HEAD WAITER *appears at the reservations lectern. He is wearing black tails*).

HEAD WAITER: Are you meeting someone, sir?

HARRY: No. He's talking to me for a moment.
> (HARRY *puts his arm round* TONY *and starts to lead him away.* STREAKY *appears from the other direction.*)

TONY: Streaky.

HARRY: Just keep walking and don't make a scene.
> (HARRY *and* STREAKY *seem both in high spirits.* STREAKY *takes a menu from the* HEAD WAITER *before following the others.*)

STREAKY: I'll take that.

TONY: What is this?

HARRY: Jungle telegraph.

STREAKY: Crikey, what a nice hotel. Three cheers for the Savoy!

HARRY: They've redone it.

STREAKY: Oh really? Was that very necessary? Was it disgusting?
> (*He is very blithe.* HARRY *has steered* TONY *towards some seats in the lobby. Now he smiles at* STREAKY.)
> (TONY *looks at them, half amused.*)

TONY: What is this?

HARRY: We heard you were having a posh dinner with the Bishop.

TONY: So I am. What of it?

HARRY: To discuss Lionel. That's what we heard.

TONY: Is the Bishop here?
> (HARRY *shakes his head.* STREAKY *has already sat down to read the menu.*)

HARRY: We thought you might like a word with us first.

46

TONY: Oh really? Why? It sounds like you don't have much confidence. If you feel you have to take me aside. It's not very flattering to Lionel.

STREAKY: I'd have half-a-dozen oysters. And follow it up with Châteaubriand. Call it a Last Supper. (*Smiles up at* TONY.) And I wonder which one are you?

(TONY *laughs, taking it in good part. Then reluctantly sits.*)

TONY: You people are shits, do you know that?

HARRY: Of course. When I was at college I had a professor who said any Christian who doesn't have a doctrine of corruption is going to find himself in all sorts of trouble. You must have a doctrine of glory as well. And your doctrine of glory must be higher. (*Looks directly at* TONY.) But only by a little bit.

(*Another* WAITER *has come and is standing next to* STREAKY.)

STREAKY: Three tequila sunrises. With cherries and umbrellas.

WAITER: Thank you, sir.

STREAKY: And the bill, if you see him, to the Bishop of Southwark.

(TONY *turns round, confused.*)

TONY: Don't bill the Bishop.

WAITER: I'm sorry, sir?

HARRY: My friend here is paying for the drinks.

(STREAKY *is counting coins on to the table in front of him.*)

STREAKY: Let me see, pieces of silver, twenty-eight, twenty-nine, thirty . . .

TONY: All right, very funny.

STREAKY: We'll pay you later.

(*The* WAITER *goes.*)

TONY: I thought you chaps came on strong about freedom. Freedom of conscience. Freedom of action. Isn't that your big thing? Let people do what they like.

HARRY: Yes. (*Pauses.*) Within a framework of loyalty.

TONY: Loyalty to each other.

HARRY: Exactly.

TONY: And the other loyalty?

(*There is a pause.* HARRY *replies with gentleness and sincerity.*)

HARRY: What, which you understand better than us?

(*The* WAITER *comes and puts down the drinks. There is a silence. No one speaks. He goes.*)

47

TONY: Look, do you think I've come here without thinking?

HARRY: No.

TONY: It's an issue of conscience.

HARRY: It always is.

TONY: I think the parish is in a very bad way. I'm shocked by this. Yes, I've heard all the familiar arguments. The Church of England's favourite text: 'Let he who is without sin cast the first stone.' All right. We can say that. We can go on saying it. We can sit where we are and say it for ever. (*Turns away, bitter.*) Does that mean no one will ever cast any stone at all?

(*There is a silence.*)

HARRY: Drink your tequila.

(TONY *shakes his head.*)

STREAKY: I'd forgotten. He's given up.

(TONY *turns and looks at them.*)

TONY: There was a woman. She'd had an abortion, I later found out. She came to Lionel for help. He faffed about as usual and sent her away. And three days later, her husband threw a pan of boiling water all over her.

(HARRY *looks across at* STREAKY.)

Yes. It's directly connected. Lionel fell down on the job.

(STREAKY *is outraged.*)

STREAKY: That's completely ridiculous.

TONY: 'Don't judge.' Honestly, that's the sum of Lionel's wisdom. Well, it won't do. He should have *judged* the danger she was in. 'Don't interfere.' 'Let them come to you . . .' Perhaps one day she will come to him. Half blinded. (*Shakes his head.*) It could have been prevented.

(HARRY *sits forward.*)

HARRY: Look, you've been here three months, you've seen the work we do . . .

STREAKY: It's one case. There are thousands.

HARRY: He's tired.

(TONY *seizes this, excited.*)

TONY: Yes. He's tired. Exactly. Lionel is tired because he gets no strength from the Gospel. That's my whole point. He's tired because he isn't getting anything back.

(HARRY *is shaking his head, disbelieving.*)

HARRY: You can't say that. How dare you? You can't say that of any priest.

TONY: Of course I can say it.

HARRY: Who are you to judge?

TONY: Have you seen him? Going down the street? In Brixton? His forehead is knotted. He gives off one message: 'Keep away. I carry the cares of the world.' It's true. People don't go near him. He reeks of personal failure. And anguish. Like so much of the church.

(HARRY *is quieter now.*)

HARRY: And you think a man should be sacked for the expression on his face? (*Smiles.*) It's a very long way from saying he looks miserable, he's ineffective, and in your view, which is extremely partial, he may be theologically unsound . . . it's a very big step to talk of these things to his bishop.

(TONY *looks at him, acknowledging the truth of his point.*)

STREAKY: No one likes to say this, Tony, but you are very young.

TONY: Yes, I know.

STREAKY: You've only just started, old chap.

TONY: It's a formula for impotence. What is this? The Civil Service? (*Smiles.*) Put in twenty years and then you can speak? (*Shakes his head.*) I went round to this woman's house.

HARRY: We heard.

TONY: I experienced this feeling of utter powerlessness. The Church can do nothing in our parish except witness to suffering. (*Looks at them, sure of himself.*) And I'm afraid I no longer think that's enough. I'm tired of standing there, wringing my hands and saying, 'Oh, this is dreadful . . .' I think we stop hedging. I think we come out with what we believe.

(HARRY *looks a moment to* STREAKY.)

HARRY: And what is that?

TONY: What it says in the Bible. Yes. Nothing more, nothing less. People must be converted. There is only one religion. Yes, one. Whatever your background. And the only way to God is through Jesus Christ. (*Pauses a moment.*) And if

49

when we say that we divide people . . . if a certain
harshness begins to creep in . . . well I'd live with that.
Because the alternative, going round smiling, sitting
people down, have a little chat, very nice, nice to see you,
arrivederci . . . that doesn't work. I've seen it. (*Smiles.*)
Christ came not to bring peace but the sword.
(HARRY *shudders.*)

HARRY: Yes, I thought you might give us that one. It's a
dangerous text. It may be corrupt. It's contested.

TONY: Any text with any life to it is now contested.
(*Before* HARRY *can answer,* TONY *rides in passionately.*)
Look, you know, I'm like you, I went along with it. For
years I was the same, I saw it your way . . .
(*The* WAITER *has reappeared next to* STREAKY.)

STREAKY: Oh God, yes, please. It's essential . . .

HARRY: And waiter . . .
(*The* WAITER *stops.*)
With extra tequila this time.
(*The* WAITER *goes.*)

TONY: I remember at college we were lectured by a bishop.
Actually he was a very decent man. They all are. Everyone
laughed at my question. I said, 'Bishop, what's the present
thinking on hell.' 'Hell?' he said. 'Yes.' He said, 'Well, we
believe in it.' I said, 'I see. Then why do we hear so little
about it? It doesn't come up much in the pulpit these
days.' He said, 'No. No we try to downplay it. After all,
we don't want to put people off . . .'
(*They all smile.*)

HARRY: All right, I agree, that's ridiculous.

TONY: Yes, you see, but it's *typical*.

HARRY: Of what?

TONY: It's an attitude, Harry. That's *Lionel*. There, in a
nutshell. Anything rather than lay out the facts. The only
effect of all his fiddle-faddle is to leave people confused.
People need rules. They actually want to be able to say,
OK, this I agree to.

HARRY: Do they?

TONY: Yes. They do. And why not? (*Smiles, at the neatness.*)
We've been *given* these rules, and by chance, what's

extremely convenient, these rules are all set down in a
book . . .

(*The* WAITER *returns with larger drinks.*)

STREAKY: Thank you, that's wonderful . . .

TONY: And this book is on sale, it's actually available . . .

HARRY: Oh yes, yes, yes . . .

(*This to the* WAITER *as he takes a huge drink from the tray.*)

TONY: You can actually take it, you can actually go and say,
what is the position on this? What is the thinking? Oh yes.
Look. John, for instance. A little line of print. 'Except a
man be born again of water and the spirit he cannot enter
into the Kingdom of God . . .'

STREAKY: I see. Well, gracious.

HARRY: You can't be serious.

(TONY *shakes his head, decisive now.*)

TONY: The whole thing's become a racket. You know it has,
Harry. Inner-city priesthood? It's a cartel. Based on a
massive failure of nerve. (*Nods.*) You've become enlightened
humanists. You do good work. I mean it. God knows,
fourteen-hour days covering for all the other community
services. But when it comes down to it, that's not the whole
message. It's got to be distinctive. People need more. They
need more than . . .

(*He censors himself, stopping in mid-sentence.*)

HARRY: Yes?

(*There's a pause.*)

They need more than what? Why not say it, Tony? You've
not spared us anything else.

(*He and* STREAKY *smile.*)

TONY: They need more than Lionel's weekly lecture on why they
should be sucking up to the poor.

(*There's a silence.*)

STREAKY: If I weren't holding this drink, then I'd sock you.

HARRY: Plainly you've travelled a very long way. Very quickly.

(TONY *looks down.*)

TONY: Yes, I have, Harry. I knew you'd be horrified . . . (*Shakes
his head.*) It isn't as if I haven't tried to change Lionel. But
he's actually stubborn. Like, for a start-off, I said the other
day, 'Look, there's this big Billy Graham crusade.' I asked,

51

'What are we going to contribute?' He said, 'Nothing. We don't like their methods.' I said, 'We can't afford to be choosy. Sometimes they do plant a seed.' He said, 'I don't need an aged American to help me.' (*Nods.*) Now that is actually racist . . .

STREAKY: Only sort of.

TONY: It's also ageist.

STREAKY: It's also remarkably good sense.

(TONY *turns, animated.*)

TONY: Yes, of course, what he means is, we won't work with Billy Graham, ugh, we *can't* work with him, because he has this habit of touching people's feelings.

HARRY: Oh, Tony . . .

TONY: Like everything in England it turns out to be a matter of class. Educated clerics don't like evangelicals, because evangelicals drink sweet sherry and keep budgerigars and have ducks in formations on their walls. (*Nods, smiling.*) Yes, and they also have the distressing downmarket habit of trying to get people emotionally involved. (*Stares at them.*) You know I'm right. And – as it happens – I went to a grammar school, I was brought up – unlike you – among all those normal, decent people who shop at Allied Carpets and are into DIY. And I don't think they should always be looked down on. And tell me, please, what is wrong in ministering to them?

(HARRY *looks at him straight.*)

HARRY: All right, then do that.

TONY: I shall. I'm going to start a Bible class.

HARRY: Good.

TONY: Midweek. In the church hall. Bible basics.

HARRY: Have you asked Lionel?

(TONY *turns and looks at him.*)

TONY: No. I haven't. Not yet. But I will. And he'll say yes. He'll let me preach something quite different to what he believes in. Won't he?

(*The three of them are all quite still now.*)

Tell me, isn't that true?

HARRY: Yes, it is.

TONY: And do we call that strength? Or is it more like

weakness? (*Smiles to himself.*) Isn't that what we've got to decide? (*Looks round a moment, then gets up, his eyes searching the lobby.*) Where is this man?

(HARRY *looks sardonically across at* STREAKY *who raises his eyebrows.*)

TONY: I suppose you haven't seen him.

STREAKY: The Bishop?

TONY: Of course . . . He hasn't been in?

HARRY: Not unless he's disguised as a Japanese tourist.

STREAKY: You'd have heard him by now. His brass balls clang as he walks.

(STREAKY *has said this with sudden, bitter gravity.* TONY *turns, standing, rather taken aback.*)

TONY: What does that mean?

(STREAKY *smiles to himself.*)

HARRY: It means he's a heavyweight.

TONY: And?

(STREAKY *looks away, darkly.*)

STREAKY: I'm saying nothing.

TONY: Why are you both so frightened I talk to him then?

(*They both look at him.*)

HARRY: Well, we're not. Go ahead.

TONY: It's not as if what I say is going to be decisive. After all, there are two of you. Why all the panic?

HARRY: It cuts both ways, Tony. It's not in your power to get Lionel the sack. Why risk the damage? (*Looks down, quiet now.*) I mean the damage to your own conscience. Why betray a friend when you don't need to?

(TONY *looks at him.*)

TONY: You tell me. Why do you think?

(HARRY *smiles.*)

HARRY: Oh, it's absolutely clear.

TONY: Why then?

HARRY: There's a dream there, Tony. Today you've expressed the dream. It's a dream that's haunted the church for two thousand years.

TONY: What's that?

(HARRY *smiles across at* STREAKY.)

HARRY: Does it have a name? It used to. In the Inquisition,

they called it something else.

TONY: I see. (*Pauses.*) What is it?

HARRY: I'd say of all temptations it's just about the most dangerous on offer. (*Smiles, at his silkiest.*) The illusion of action.

(*And at once striding towards them come the two bishops,* KINGSTON *and* SOUTHWARK. *They both have wet hair and are looking highly energetic.*)

SOUTHWARK: Walk on, walk on, go ahead. After you, Gilbert.

HARRY: And, at last, here comes your chance. (*Gets up to greet them.*)

STREAKY: My God, double purple!

SOUTHWARK: We were detained, I'm sorry.

(HARRY *is up, but* STREAKY *is having trouble getting out of his chair.*)

STREAKY: And in off the black!

SOUTHWARK: Gilbert took me to play squash. Then we lost track of time in the Turkish bath. Goodness, there are more than I was expecting.

(STREAKY *is rising, a little uncertainly.*)

HARRY: Take no notice of my friend, he's drunk as a lord.

(SOUTHWARK *laughs and reaches out to embrace* HARRY.)

SOUTHWARK: How are you, Harry? It's so long since I saw you. I miss you, you know.

HARRY: Well, thank you, Charlie. I miss you too.

(*They hold the embrace, full of fondness, looking into each other's eyes with real warmth.* TONY *frowns, puzzled.*)

Unfortunately, I'm not saying for supper. Much as I would like to. Nor is Streaky.

STREAKY: No way, Ray.

SOUTHWARK: What's been going on?

HARRY: Oh, we've been talking to our young friend.

(*He gestures towards the hitherto ignored* TONY.)

SOUTHWARK: Yes, I thought I might question him. On inner-city problems. At the grass roots.

HARRY: Well, I hope we haven't exhausted him. He's bursting with ideas. He belongs to what I shall now call the Savoy school of theology.

(*He winks at* TONY, *who stands, lost for a reaction to all this bonhomie.*)

The Grill Room school, shall we say?

(*There is a moment's pause. All still. Then*) He'll explain to you.

SOUTHWARK: Will he?

HARRY: By all means, go on.

(SOUTHWARK *smiles.* HARRY *is now looking intently at* TONY.)

SOUTHWARK: Well, I'm sure he'll have a great deal to tell us. Say goodbye to your colleagues, then follow us.

(*This last to* TONY, *as* SOUTHWARK *turns to* KINGSTON *and they head towards the doors.*)

Now, Gilbert, where are we? It's in my name.

WAITER: I have a table by the window, my Lord.

(*The two of them vanish into the dining-room.* TONY *is left rooted to the spot, unable to move.* HARRY *and* STREAKY *are staring at him.*)

HARRY: Go on then, Tony. To your supper. (*Suddenly raises an arm.*) 'With this shining sword . . .'

(TONY *does not move.*)

Go on. What's holding you?

(TONY *stands still, not moving, agonized.*)

Go on then, Tony. Make up your mind.

SCENE TWO

The church. The middle of the night. STREAKY *enters, carrying a single candle in the dark. He walks with elaborate care. He smiles.*

STREAKY: Drunk, Lord, drunk.

And blissfully happy. Can't help it. Love the job. Love my work. Look at other people in total bewilderment. I got to drink at the Savoy. It was wonderful. It's all wonderful. Why can't people enjoy what they have?

Is it just a matter of temperament? I mean, I'm a happy priest. Always have been. Ever since I got my first job as curate at St Anselms, Cheam, because they needed a light tenor for the parochial Gilbert and Sullivan society. Matins, a sung Eucharist, two Evensongs and *Iolanthe* five nights a week.

55

It was bliss. I loved it. I tried to start it here. But there's something deep in the Jamaican character that can't find its way through *The Pirates of Penzance*. It's still bliss, though. They are blissful people. Once a year we take the coach to the sea. On the way down we have the rum and the curried goat. Lord, there is no end to your goodness. Then we have rum and curried goat on the way back.

Lord, I have no theology. Can't do it. By my bed, there's a pile of paperbacks called *The Meaning of Meaning*, and *How to Ask Why*. They've been there for years. The whole thing's so clear. You're there. In people's happiness. Tonight, in the taste of that drink. Or the love of my friends. The whole thing's so simple. Infinitely loving.

Why do people find it so hard?

SCENE THREE

Lionel's house. There is a table and a chessboard on it. A warm light near it. FRANCES *and* LIONEL *are playing chess opposite each other. He is out of his dog collar, in slacks and a Viyella shirt. She is in jeans. It is quiet, intimate and warm.*

FRANCES: Please play the game.
    (*He puts his hand on a piece.*)
    You can't do that. If you do that you're checkmate in three.
LIONEL: I don't want to play.
FRANCES: You have to.
LIONEL: I'd like to pace up and down.
FRANCES: Well, you can't.
    (*She smiles.*)
LIONEL: How come you're so good at it? Are you good at everything?
FRANCES: No.
LIONEL: What are you bad at?
FRANCES: Just move your knight there.
LIONEL: (*Doing it*) There?

56

FRANCES: That's a good move.
    (*He shakes his head.*)
LIONEL: I'm sorry. I had no right to ring you. It's not as if we're close.
FRANCES: We're close. In understanding.
    (LIONEL *sits back.*)
LIONEL: It's funny. I think of myself as part of the community.
FRANCES: (*Frowns*) Hold on. Let me think.
LIONEL: The chap in the paper shop. All the school caretakers. These are my friends. There's a lovely woman who runs the charity shop. All the sidesmen. The wardens. Harry. And Streaky, of course. And yet – I don't know – when I was standing in the hospital this morning, I thought, I don't know a soul.
    (*He stares at her.*)
FRANCES: She'll be fine. (*Returns to looking at the board, then reassures him.*) It's all right.
    (*He looks away.*)
LIONEL: She was lying there half an hour.
FRANCES: What do you mean?
LIONEL: You see I was in my study, working on my sermon. She fell in the kitchen. I heard nothing. It was so typical. So when the ambulance came, I was ashamed to say, 'Well, actually, look, this is awful, I don't know how long she's been there . . .'
    (*She looks across at him.*)
FRANCES: They let her out, Lionel. It's nothing. It couldn't have been milder. It's a very slight stroke.
    (LIONEL *nods. Without much forethought his hand involuntarily moves a piece.*)
FRANCES: Oh, really, Lionel . . .
LIONEL: What?
FRANCES: Look, just look . . . (*Points to two other pieces.*) There. And there. What's wrong with you? Are you suicidal? Do you have some sort of deathwish?
LIONEL: Yes. I'm sorry.
    (*He reaches out and for a moment it looks as if he will touch her cheek. But he stops just short. Then he smiles and withdraws his hand.*)

I'm out of my class.

(*She looks down.*)

FRANCES: Did you find Alex?

LIONEL: Yes. I managed to get hold of him. He's on holiday in France. He's coming back.

FRANCES: And Lucy?

LIONEL: No. (*Pause.*) It's difficult. We don't have an address. It's very hard on Heather. (*Shrugs.*) I must say, it is odd. I know so many clergy families where the children have gone. They seem to get very angry. Was it like that for you?

FRANCES: A bit. I mean, of course I was angry for a while.

LIONEL: Yes. Why is that?

(*She pauses for a moment.*)

FRANCES: Because it all seems such a waste.

LIONEL: What kind of waste?

FRANCES: Of a human being. To have his mind all the time on something else. Always to be dreaming.

LIONEL: Is that how it seems?

FRANCES: Well, yes, it does.

(*He is thoughtful, quiet, as if this has hit home.*)

Is that so for Lucy?

(*He looks at her a moment.*)

LIONEL: I really can't say.

(FRANCES *waits a second.*)

FRANCES: If I were a clergyman what I'd find unbearable is to have to talk about what I believe. Press a button and a clergyman's duty-bound to tell me. At once. Even if he doesn't know me very well. He has to tell me his innermost belief. (*Smiles.*) That's what's undignified. That's why clergymen are funny, I'm afraid. Because they're not allowed to be private. They wear their inside on their outside.

LIONEL: Oh, do you think?

FRANCES: I only know what's most important is those things no one can speak of.

(*He is watching her closely.*)

LIONEL: And what things are they?

FRANCES: In my life?

58

LIONEL: Yes.

(*She smiles again, very light.*)

FRANCES: Oh, odd moments. Watching. Thinking. The way you feel love.

(LIONEL *watches her, she is deep in thought.*)

LIONEL: And are you really leaving?

FRANCES: Soon. I want to work abroad. I'm from a missionary family. It just happens I don't have the faith. (*Laughs.*) I have an idea of countries where things have value. Because life is hard. Our agency represents this charity, you see. They'll fix it for me. I'm sorry. I know I sound pi.

LIONEL: Not at all.

FRANCES: But if you want a real life now, where else do you go?

(*He is sitting very still, rapt. She smiles.*)

It makes me laugh the way you don't even mention him.

LIONEL: Who?

FRANCES: God.

LIONEL: Oh, that's not fair. I do sometimes. I find myself calling him 'God, as it were'. Who has a son called 'Jesus, as it were'. It's true. I'm embarrassed. So I apologize. 'As it were'.

(FRANCES *grins.*)

The moment you start using all the language, you distance people. And it's not important. He's there. He loves people whether they know it or not.

(FRANCES *nods.*)

So much of what passes for religion is simply nonsense. Close the church doors and all tell God how wonderful he is. Where does that get you? And the more people doing it, the more you're said to be thriving. It's phoney. (*Shakes his head.*) It doesn't connect. The doors should be open. A priest should be like any other man. Only full of God's love.

(*He is looking intently across the table at her.*)

FRANCES: And is that possible?

LIONEL: I have no idea.

(*The door opens and* HEATHER *is standing there. She is wearing only a nightgown and looks deathly pale. She is totally disorientated.*)

HEATHER: What's this?

LIONEL: You're out of bed.

HEATHER: I heard voices.

(LIONEL *has shot up, guiltily and is about to move towards her. But she is now staring at* FRANCES, *who is frozen to her chair.*)

LIONEL: You must go back to bed.

(*But she is fixed on* FRANCES. *She does not waver. She looks insane.*)

HEATHER: I don't know you.

FRANCES: We did meet.

LIONEL: Heather, this is Frances Parnell.

(*She goes on staring then turns and looks at* LIONEL.)

She came to sit with me.

(HEATHER *looks at him as if the words are completely meaningless.*)

Yes.

HEATHER: That's very good of you.

LIONEL: Heather, please.

(*He panics, ushering her from the room, his arm round her, guiding her.*)

Look, em, goodness. Sorry. Excuse me. Heather, you must go back to bed.

(*They go out. There is a moment. And then* FRANCES *gets up and pulls on her jacket, coat and scarf. She is about to go as* LIONEL *appears from the room.*)

What are you doing?

FRANCES: I'm off.

LIONEL: Look . . .

FRANCES: Stay with her, Lionel. You must sit in the room. You can see she doesn't know what's happening.

(*He is staring at her as if he didn't understand.*)

Lionel, she's in the most terrible state.

LIONEL: You don't have to go.

FRANCES: Yes I do.

LIONEL: Why? I put her back to bed.

FRANCES: That's not the point.

LIONEL: But it's innocent.

(*She looks at him a moment.*)

FRANCES: Yes. Partly it is, and partly it's not.
(*He looks at her a moment then moves towards her.*)
LIONEL: No, listen to me, Frances . . .
FRANCES: I can't. Please. Say nothing, Lionel. You know
what's going on. It's nice, of course. I enjoy it. Sitting
here, playing chess. Letting you imagine. (*Looks down.*)
Honestly, now I'm being unkind.
LIONEL: No. It's true.
FRANCES: But it isn't real.
(*Before he can speak she interrupts.*)
Don't be stupid. You have a sick wife. (*Smiles.*) You're
not allowed any pleasure. Except the pleasure of dreaming.
(*They both smile. Then she crosses the room and kisses him on
the cheek.*)
LIONEL: Bless you.
FRANCES: I'll see you soon.

SCENE FOUR

A darkened street. HARRY *going home, in an overcoat, his keys
already in his hand as he approaches the front door of a small
terraced house.* TOMMY ADAIR *steps out of the shadows, smoking a
cigarette.*

HARRY: Hello.
TOMMY: I needed a vicar. I needed someone to talk about sin.
So I thought I'd come to an expert.
HARRY: Are you in trouble? Do you mean now? (*Frowns.*) If
it's not urgent we can make an appointment.
TOMMY: That'll be too late. I need to be sorted out by Sunday.
HARRY: Sunday? (*Looks closely at* TOMMY.) Do you mean
before church? (*Starts to move away, suspicious.*) Why don't
you ring in the morning? My number's in the book.
TOMMY: Don't fancy me, eh?
(HARRY *gets it.*)
HARRY: Not in the slightest. Good night.
(*But* TOMMY *at once goes on to the attack, raising his voice
for the first time.*)

61

TOMMY: I'm from a well-known national newspaper. I talked
with a great friend of yours. He's rather a sweet and
passive boy.

(HARRY *just looks, not answering.*)

I'm doing an investigative piece. It'll appear next Sunday.
If we talked you could give me a number of other names.
And that way your own name might not appear.

(*There is a pause. Then* HARRY *moves towards him, casual,
not frightened, taking him on.*)

HARRY: I'll send you the synodical paper on exactly the subject
you're interested in. Yes. The church set up a committee
some years ago. A report was commissioned. I can let you
have a copy if you like. If you have space you can print it
in full. Did you know we had a synodical debate? Are you
a theological correspondent?

(HARRY *moves closer to him.*)

The report asserts that genital acts between men are not
necessarily wrong. Do you know those words?
'Necessarily'? 'Genital'?

(TOMMY *is unamused.*)

TOMMY: I wouldn't advise you to be aggressive. You're not in
a strong position.

HARRY: In fact I am. (*Smiles, confident.*) You see my big
strength is, I don't believe you. No friend of mine would
have spoken to you. And anyway, my life is between me
and God. And God, as I may best comprehend him, does
not work through the Sunday papers. (*Smiles.*) Not at least
if He's who I think He is. (*Makes to go.*)

TOMMY: You're digging your own grave.

HARRY: I'll risk that.

TOMMY: (*Shrugs*) It makes no difference.

HARRY: Then go ahead. Good luck. (*Turns and reaches the steps
of his house.*)

TOMMY: Shall I give your love to Ewan?

(*For the first time* HARRY *stops, his back to us. There is just a
moment's pause in his step. Then he carries on into the house.*)

HARRY: By all means. Do what you like.

The church. HARRY *comes in, in his overcoat. He stands a moment, alone in the dark.*

HARRY: Lord, I don't know. Of course I'm frightened. What would you expect? But I won't sink to their level.

I won't speak to Ewan. I trust him. Everything's fine.

I've always been proud that I have no illusions. In the three years I was at Cambridge I only kissed a man once. By the river actually. In the darkness. I couldn't see his face. It still dazzles me, the memory. The three years weren't wasted because . . . there was this single moment of unbelievable happiness. Lord, you know I don't expect more.

We get by on so little. We all wore flannels. And herringbone jackets. The joke is, I still do. We smoked pipes. Long evenings spent discussing Teildhard de Chardhin, and thinking what's his body like under the tweed?

I'm clear-eyed. I think I am. There is people as they are. And there is people as they could be. The priest's job is to try and yank the two a little bit closer. It takes a good deal of time.

People have souls. That man from the newspaper, even. I have to remember. It's my duty. But I also have a duty to fight.

Oh God, please help me. I don't understand. Teach me. How do you fight without hate?

SCENE SIX

A bitter, windy day. There is an enormous billboard, eighteen feet long and eight feet high. A chic, strapless model lies on her side, advertising a women's magazine, with a cute strapline. In front of the hoarding, TONY *waits in a duffel coat. Then* FRANCES *appears, in jeans and coat.*

TONY: So it is you.

FRANCES: Yes.

TONY: I thought it might be.

(*There's a pause.*)

FRANCES: How are you, Tony?

TONY: I'm well. And you?

(*She looks at him a moment.*)

FRANCES: Well, give me a kiss.

TONY: I'm sorry.

(*He kisses her cheek, then gestures towards the enormous hoarding.*)

So this is it.

FRANCES: Yes.

TONY: This is our first poster site. (*Looks up at it admiringly.*) Can we have any message we want?

FRANCES: No. There's a drafting committee for the trial area. My uncle said, 'I hear there's a bright young man in Brixton.' I said, 'Yes.' He said, 'Let's get him in.'

TONY: I'm flattered. (*Smiles, shifting from foot to foot.*) I'm bursting with ideas. I love the size of it, don't you? Wham! It'll be like saying Christ really belongs. Not just in church. But in the high street. Why not? It's what we need. To shake the fuddy-duddy image. (*Smiles.*) Real resources. A really modern campaign.

(*FRANCES is just watching him, not speaking. He steals a quick glance at her, then goes on, enthusiastically.*)

It's going well here. I've started a Bible class. We've had the first three. We've doubled our numbers each week. It's inspiring. People come. All races. All backgrounds. You know. They love listening to scripture. Then we discuss it. People have got so used to thinking Christianity's difficult. But read the Bible and they find it's quite easy.

(*FRANCES nods slightly*)

FRANCES: And what does Lionel think?

TONY: Lionel? (*Shrugs slightly.*) I don't know. I don't really see him.

FRANCES: Why not?

TONY: He's been involved with problems of his own. (*A pause.*) Heather was ill.

FRANCES: I heard that.

TONY: Also . . .

(*He stops.*)

FRANCES: Yes?

TONY: The Bishop is trying to get rid of him. Lionel is
threatening to make the most tremendous stink. It's not
very easy. Being in my position. They even asked me for
my opinion. I was called in once. They wanted my view.

FRANCES: And did you give it?

TONY: Of course. I think honesty's important. (*Slight pause.*
He's quiet.) You know me, Frances. You know I think
that.

(FRANCES *just looks at him.*)

We're dealing with a man who's in desperate trouble.

FRANCES: Lionel?

TONY: Go round the parish. Ask anyone. I mean, I wish it
weren't true.

FRANCES: What kind of trouble?

(TONY *smiles.*)

TONY: Apart from anything, why do you think Heather had a
stroke?

FRANCES: I don't know.

(TONY *is shaking his head.*)

You tell me.

TONY: His daughter ran away. Have you ever talked to her? She
has a problem of alcohol addiction. She's not even nineteen.
She despises him. She says he's given her nothing as a father.
(*Nods.*) God is trying to say something to Lionel.

FRANCES: Really? (*Waits.*) And? *What* is he saying?

TONY: Well, I think it's pretty clear. In the gentlest possible way.
He's giving him a hint. (*Looks at her, then smiles slightly.*) I
mean, why else would he strike Heather down?

FRANCES: I don't know.

(TONY *moves away.*)

TONY: I mean, don't get me wrong, God isn't a mechanic, with a
screwdriver, who comes along and tampers with the machine
from the outside. It's not like that. Things develop inside
human beings. And sometimes these things are dangerously
wrong.

65

FRANCES: God drops a hint?

TONY: Yes.

FRANCES: That's his method?

TONY: I think it is. He does certain things. And we must draw
the right conclusions.

(FRANCES *is watching him dispassionately*.)

FRANCES: And you think he's telling Lionel it's time to go?

(TONY *shrugs*.)

TONY: It's not for me to say. Lionel must decide that. I don't
pontificate on individuals.

FRANCES: Don't you?

TONY: No, of course not. You must always stop short of that.
(*Nods sincerely*.) It's Lionel's decision. But you know, if he
goes on as he is, things can only get worse for him. Unless
... (*Stops*.)

FRANCES: Unless?

TONY: Unless he changes his life.

FRANCES: Changes it?

TONY: Yes. (*Nods*.) I do mean that. It's incredibly ironic. My
own conversion – the true one, I mean – happened way
after I was actually ordained. I felt this complete
overturning. Of everything. God told me what I was here
for. It was as if I'd never heard him. (*Turns and looks at
her*.) And since then I have this incredible power. (*Smiles*.)
Oh, I'm still me. I'm Tony. I'm the same bloke. But now
I can throw on three extra generators. Whoosh! It's
extraordinary. Whenever I want.

(*She watches him. He is completely confident*.)

That can still happen to Lionel. I pray for it. He just
needs to ask himself 'What's happening to me? Why have
I got nothing but problems? I mean, what is God trying to
say to me here?'

FRANCES: What, you think there's a reason for his suffering?

TONY: Of course. Human beings can choose. We're free.
Notice the message. Or ignore it. Ignore it and pay a
terrible price.

(FRANCES *nods*.)

FRANCES: I see. (*Very quiet*.) This God of yours ...

TONY: Yes?

66

FRANCES: He killed your parents.

(TONY *frowns, hurt.*)

TONY: Frances . . .

FRANCES: No, look, I'm serious.

TONY: It was an accident.

FRANCES: But?

(TONY *looks at her, reluctant to reply.*)

But *what*? I'm really asking. What was he trying to say
then?

TONY: He was giving me a shock.

FRANCES: A shock?

TONY: Yes. I know now. That was the point of it. I've no
doubt the whole thing was directed at me.

FRANCES: How?

TONY: He wanted to shake me up. To set me on a path which
leads here. Via you. Via my conversion. To my Bible class
and all my future work in this parish. To everything now
which is good and worthwhile.

(FRANCES *turns away.*)

FRANCES: And for you to get your shock, you're saying your
own parents died?

(TONY *shakes his head, bewildered.*)

TONY: No. Don't be ridiculous. I mean, also he needed them.

FRANCES: Needed them?

TONY: Yes. (*Quietly.*) It was their time.

FRANCES: On an icy motorway?

TONY: Yes.

FRANCES: Deserted? At night?

TONY: Yes. As it happened.

(*There's a silence. Then he turns and looks at her.*)

Well, what other reason can there be? (*Turns away.*) Of
course at the time I didn't understand it.

FRANCES: You didn't. No.

TONY: Not at all. How could I?

FRANCES: You were wild.

TONY: I was. I was bewildered.

FRANCES: You used to wake in the night and make love to me.

(*He looks at her.*)

TONY: Yes I did.

FRANCES: Crying all the time.

TONY: Yes, that's right.

(*There's a silence. The grief is in the air.*)

He makes us suffer. Through suffering we learn. (*Looks at her, then shakes his head, smiling to himself.*) How can I have been so stupid? I used to try and find comfort in you.

FRANCES: Try?

TONY: In your body. It was crazy. I realize now I was wasting my time. (*Nods, then smiles at her to reassure her.*) I mean, please be clear, you were so kind to me . . .

(*But she turns, having trouble asking him what she most wants to know.*)

FRANCES: Tony. In bed you used to say certain things.

TONY: Did I?

FRANCES: Yes.

TONY: Good gracious.

FRANCES: Do you remember?

TONY: Sort of. (*Shrugs and shuffles, being cheeky.*) You know.

FRANCES: Were those things true?

TONY: I *thought* they were true at the time. That's my point.

(*She turns away.*)

Don't be hurt. Why be hurt, Frances? It's a fact. Human love passes. God's love doesn't. (*Frowns.*) Can't you find comfort in that?

(FRANCES *is overwhelmed for a moment, fighting tears.*)

FRANCES: No, I can't.

TONY: You should.

FRANCES: I find it disgusting. It's here. We live here. On this earth. That's where we have to love one another. (*Suddenly savage.*) Tell me, what did you say to the Bishop that night?

TONY: The Bishop?

FRANCES: Yes.

TONY: What's that to do with it?

FRANCES: When he asked you what you thought of Lionel? What answer did you give?

(*He shakes his head, angry already.*)

TONY: It really annoys me . . .

68

FRANCES: Why?

TONY: That's all anyone asks me.

FRANCES: Well?

TONY: No one asks, 'How are the people out there? Are they getting what they need from us?' Oh no, it's just, 'I say old chap, did you let the side down?' Well as it happens I didn't go to public school. So appeals to public-school morality mean nothing to me.

(*She stands, still waiting for her answer.*)

FRANCES: So?

(*He shifts uneasily.*)

TONY: Frances, I'm altered.

FRANCES: Yes, I can see that.

TONY: You don't understand. It's all irrelevant. Lionel's in the past.

FRANCES: In the past for *you*.

TONY: I have accepted a supernatural religion. Since I did that, everything has changed. (*He smiles, shaking his head.*) You know, all around everyone is screaming. 'Lionel! Lionel!' all the time. It's just become total gibberish to me, the word itself doesn't make any sense . . . (*Tries it out, shouting it.*) 'Lionel!' (*Shakes his head.*) All I can see is a man who's missing the obvious. Christ intervened. Lionel doesn't seem to realize. Two thousand years ago. There was an intervention. (*Suddenly impassioned now.*) And when God did this, when he sent his own son, then he offered a model, it was a promise, if you like, to all the rest of us. No one need be bound by the rules of reality . . .

FRANCES: Oh, look, Tony, come on . . .

TONY: He was saying, 'Look, if you don't want them, the rules don't apply . . .'

(FRANCES *is standing just watching now, bewildered by* TONY's *sudden access of energy.*)

FRANCES: What do you *mean*?

(*But* TONY *is already smiling, ahead of her.*)

TONY: Oh yes, I know what you're thinking. You think psychologically. So you think something's happened. 'Oh, Tony's lonely. That's it. He's in grief. There's an

explanation. He misses his parents.' 'Hey', even, 'he
misses *me . . .*' (*Looks triumphantly at her.*) Well, all that
stuff, it's just a load of nonsense. All that matters is that
I'm healed.

(*He reacts at once to her disbelief.*)

FRANCES: Healed?

TONY: Yes! Read the Bible, for goodness' sake. Analyse. What
does Jesus actually do? Most of the time? He heals. And
mostly in public. In the marketplace.

FRANCES: Tony, is this what you want to do?

(TONY *moves towards her, already on to the next thing.*)

TONY: No, look, I tell you, I know you won't believe this.
Keep an open mind. It's a fact. There's an AIDS patient
. . . no, listen, it's true. It's in Kilburn. A Christian
brotherhood sent me the gen. I've got the stuff.

(*There's a pause.*)

He had AIDS. Now he doesn't.

FRANCES: Tony, you're going out of your head.

TONY: No, I'm not.

FRANCES: This is sick. How dare you?

TONY: (*He is shaking his head.*) I will let you see the
documents.

FRANCES: This is immoral.

TONY: I will tell you how they did it. With some oil. And the
power of prayer. (*Pauses, challenging her.*) Come back with
me and I will give you his name.

FRANCES: I don't want to come back with you.

TONY: I can show you a photocopy of the tests. There is
medical data. It is signed by doctors.

FRANCES: So what?

(*He smiles.*)

TONY: No, you can't say that. There's proof. It's an
intervention. The virus has gone.

(FRANCES *just watches him now.*)

What were they calling it? 'The scourge of the world'?
You've read the newspapers. 'The plague of mankind'?
And now we know . . . like that . . . (*Flicks his fingers.*)
A man may be transformed. (*Nods, quiet now. He turns to
her, bubbling over now, excited, flushed.*) I have to keep it

70

down, it's hilarious, I tell you. I get on a bus, I'm sitting there, I think . . . 'A virgin gave birth.' It's supernatural. Why do we forget that? I become so excited. On the bus, with all the other passengers, it's crazy. I have to hide the smile on my face. I can't believe it. (*Looks at her. Then as if saying the words for the first time.*) 'Then a corpse walked out of a tomb . . .' (*Stands a moment, content.*) Lionel, indeed! What does it matter? If he could just see . . . I mean *really* see . . . then he could share in this power. (FRANCES *looks at him a moment.*) Why not? Tell me why not? (*She turns and walks away from him. Then she begins to run.* TONY *stands a moment, pained. Then firmly.*) Frances! Frances! Come back!

SCENE SEVEN

The church. STELLA *has a patch over the glass on one of her spectacles, and her skin is scalded on one side of her face. She has a bucket and mop.*

STELLA: Lord, this is crazy. £2.50 an hour? D'un seem to me religious. It's very unreligious.

I'll do this for now. I e'n't doin' it for long.

I din' want this. I din' want any of it. He lost 'is temper, that's all. He lost it for one moment. He threw a pan at me. All right. But it was just one moment. You ask me what's Christian? I thought the Christian thing was to forgive.

But I'm not allowed to. I 'ad to leave. They said, you're livin' with a dangerous man. And I keep sayin', yes, 'e's dangerous now, 'cos 'e's so frightened. Jus' leave us alone. And that way, we'll 'ave a chance.

I'm never goin' to testify. Whatever Tony tells me. Against my own husband. It was my life.

I liked those days in the big bed when we din' get up. We ate and drank and watched television. Once three days went by. And 'e was great.

71

I'm just waiting. And then I'm going to get my life
back.

SCENE EIGHT

*The crypt of the cathedral. At once the low tolling of a bell for a
service.* LIONEL *stands alone, waiting, in black cassock. There is a
chair. Servers come and go.* GILBERT KINGSTON *arrives, busily.
His manner is sober. He is dressed in purple.*

KINGSTON: Yes, Lionel, good.

LIONEL: Gilbert.

KINGSTON: Welcome. The Bishop will not have long.

LIONEL: I see.

(*There's a pause.*)

KINGSTON: It's a bad time.

LIONEL: Yes.

KINGSTON: For the Bishop. Things could hardly be more
grave. He will preach a sermon at the sung Eucharist. He
plans to say he is no longer in communion with the other
bishops who have done this.

(LIONEL *waits, saying nothing.*)

It's a time of great anguish. I have to ask you not to make
matters worse.

(*Robes arrive for the Bishop, on a rack, with mitre, etc.*)

Just present your argument. You're in the middle of your
work.

LIONEL: Yes.

KINGSTON: You have planted seeds, which will bear fruit later.

LIONEL: Yes.

KINGSTON: You're re-examining your methods.

LIONEL: Yes.

KINGSTON: You admit perhaps in the past . . . (*Stops.*)

LIONEL: Yes?

KINGSTON: Your own attitudes obscured your approach to the
community. But now you have a very strong team.
Particularly a recent brilliant recruit. The Bishop likes
him.

LIONEL: I see.

72

KINGSTON: He finds him dynamic.

(*There's a pause.*)

LIONEL: Well, he is.

(KINGSTON *looks at him a moment.*)

KINGSTON: Please, Lionel, no hint of reservation. Be humble. I beg of you. Play this low key.

(SOUTHWARK *arrives with characteristic gravity. He is attended by* DRESSERS *and* SERVERS. *The two men waiting make way. Then* SOUTHWARK *is still.*)

SOUTHWARK: Lionel. (*Pauses as if he might say something, but then turns.*) I must dress while we're talking.

(*The* ATTENDANTS *set to work, laying out his clothes, then robing him.*)

I assume you've heard the news.

LIONEL: Indeed.

SOUTHWARK: In my soul, I had never believed this could happen. Where will it end?

LIONEL: You tell me, Charlie.

SOUTHWARK: Christ came as a man. His chosen disciples were men. The priesthood has been occupied by men for two thousand years. A woman was given a very different function. A higher function, even. To be the mother of Christ. Are we saying we now give in to every fad and fashion? Every passing cultural upheaval? (*Turns and looks* LIONEL *in the eye.*) On the other side of the Atlantic they have put rochet and chimere on a woman's body.

(*There is a pause.*)

The Church of England is about what you can stomach.

LIONEL: I understand that.

SOUTHWARK: And I've reached the stage where I can stomach no more.

(*He ignores the waiting* SERVER, *instead holding his look to* LIONEL.)

And you?

LIONEL: Me?

SOUTHWARK: You did as I asked you?

LIONEL: Yes.

SOUTHWARK: You went to Slough?

(LIONEL *pauses a second.*)

73

LIONEL: Yes.

SOUTHWARK: How was it?

(LIONEL *pauses again, looking to* KINGSTON.)

KINGSTON: Go on, Lionel, please.

(*There is a slight pause.*)

LIONEL: It was a series of housing estates on the edge of a
sewage farm. Jets go overhead every few minutes.

(SOUTHWARK *looks to* KINGSTON *a moment.*)

SOUTHWARK: Do I take it your answer is no?

(LIONEL *looks uneasily but before he can really reply*
KINGSTON *rides in on top of him.*)

LIONEL: Well actually . . .

KINGSTON: It's a bad day for Charlie.

LIONEL: Yes, I know.

KINGSTON: We're talking about a woman Bishop.

LIONEL: Yes, quite.

KINGSTON: Inside the Anglican Communion.

SOUTHWARK: It seems, if I may say so, in the scale of things
rather more important than your egotism.

(LIONEL *looks at him, wary of responding.*)

Am I to be detained by one man's vanity? In anticipation of
today I already have three sacks of mail.

LIONEL: I understand. But perhaps it was unwise to try and see
me in these circumstances.

SOUTHWARK: I want the matter settled.

LIONEL: Yes. (*Looks at* SOUTHWARK *pitilessly.*) I can tell.

(*There's a moment. Then* SOUTHWARK *turns to his*
ATTENDANTS.)

SOUTHWARK: Leave us.

ATTENDANT: My Lord, they're ready for you now.

SOUTHWARK: Leave me. Please.

(*The* ATTENDANTS *go.* SOUTHWARK *is thoughtful, then speaks
as if they were still there.*)

SOUTHWARK: They must wait. (*Looks at* LIONEL *a moment.*) Do
you know how many parishioners come to a bishop and say
'Our parish priest is useless. There's no inspiration. The
congregation despair of him. What can you do?' And I have to
say 'Nothing. You are stuck with him. That is the rule of the
Church of England. There is absolutely nothing I can do.'

LIONEL: Has there been a delegation?

(SOUTHWARK *ignores this*.)

SOUTHWARK: In my view you're bad at your job because people can't get hold of you.

LIONEL: I see.

SOUTHWARK: They have no idea what you believe. Your answer to everything is to say 'Well it's complex . . .'

LIONEL: It *is* complex.

SOUTHWARK: Any specific question they ask you: 'Do you believe Christ ascended into heaven?' 'Oh, well, it depends what you mean . . .' (*Smiles*.) And all at once, you've lost them. Because you don't say yes, I believe in the following things. The Virgin Birth. The Resurrection. The thirty-nine articles. Etcetera. Whatever. The Athanasian Creed. (*Turns to* LIONEL *directly*.) I asked you to my house. Do you remember?

LIONEL: Yes.

SOUTHWARK: We gave you an excellent lunch.

LIONEL: That's right.

SOUTHWARK: You said you no longer believed in the importance of the sacraments . . .

LIONEL: Did I say that? Those words exactly?

SOUTHWARK: I gave you a warning. You took no heed. (*Looks quickly to* KINGSTON.) From that day on, you were dead.

LIONEL: Dead?

(LIONEL *frowns, as if thinking about this.* KINGSTON *shifts uneasily at the bluntness. There is no apology in* SOUTHWARK's *manner*.)

SOUTHWARK: Oh yes, it's cruel. I do understand that. I am not unfeeling. But I also have a charge. I am duty-bound to decide where the line must be drawn. (*Nods*.) No two people will ever agree on theology. It's not possible. You can't make decrees about the meaning of Holy Scripture. But you can insist that, whatever our beliefs, we assemble together and perform the same rituals.

LIONEL: I agree. As long as those rituals aren't an organized hypocrisy.

SOUTHWARK: Yes. I know you think that. (*Looks at him thoughtfully*.) But what else can we do? Truly? (*Shrugs*.)

75

People *are* different. It's a fact. They hold different views. We cannot comprehend God. If we could, we would not be here. When we understand him, we shall be in heaven. (*Pauses a moment, thinking about it.*) So meanwhile we must rely on formulae which have served men well for two thousand years. No, more than rely on them. I have begun lately to realize we must fight for them as well. (*Looks at* LIONEL.) It isn't my fault. I'm being pushed. Oh yes, the church's reformers are always great advocates of passion and – what do you call it? – 'commitment'. But always in their own cause. They don't like it when we become passionate back.

(LIONEL *looks, beginning to understand.* SOUTHWARK *nods.*)

LIONEL: I see.

SOUTHWARK: Yes.

LIONEL: What? And I am the sacrifice? Yes? Is that right? To what end? To encourage the others?

(SOUTHWARK *does not answer.*)

Do you have a replacement?

SOUTHWARK: I'm sorry?

LIONEL: A new team Rector? Do you have someone lined up?

SOUTHWARK: I do.

LIONEL: Who?

(KINGSTON *looks nervously at* SOUTHWARK *as if hoping he won't answer.*)

SOUTHWARK: You wouldn't know him. He's an excellent chap. I was at school with his father.

LIONEL: Oh well, it's open and shut.

SOUTHWARK: He's a natural leader. The gospel is in him. He looks outside himself. There is no cleft in his brow. He is not in permanent pain.

(LIONEL *looks at him.*)

LIONEL: And have you fixed it already?

SOUTHWARK: I didn't hear you.

LIONEL: Have you told him he has the job?

(*There is a pause.* SOUTHWARK *looks at him, as if judging him, as* KINGSTON *looks away, compromised. Then* SOUTHWARK *shakes his head, as if coming to a conclusion about* LIONEL.)

SOUTHWARK: You did it, you know. You can't pretend
    otherwise. You bring it on yourselves. All of you.
    Modernists. You make all these changes. You force all
    these issues. The remarriage of clergy. The recognition of
    homosexual love. New Bibles. New services. You alter the
    form. You dismantle the beliefs. You endlessly reinterpret
    and undermine. You witter on, till you become all things
    to all men. You drain religion of religion. And then you're
    so bound up in your own self-righteousness you affect
    astonishment when some of us suddenly say no. (*Pause.*)
    Well, we are saying no. You've politicized everything.
    Your wretched synod means exactly that. The church has
    been turned into a ghastly parody of government. (*Nods
    and smiles.*) And now – suddenly – you look round and
    decide you don't like the result.
    (LIONEL *is shaking his head.*)
LIONEL: That isn't fair. These things are nothing to do with
    me. I'm not even active. I'm just one more parish priest.
    (SOUTHWARK *looks as if he doesn't believe him.*)
    Well, it's true, Charlie. Really. Who, for some reason, has
    become an obsession in your head.
    (*It is suddenly quiet now.*)
SOUTHWARK: You're not an obsession.
LIONEL: No, really, it's so. This is what interests me. See it
    my way round. It's been jolly hard. Why me? Am I really
    worse than all the others? Is it arbitrary? (*Smiles.*) I've
    heard you say you want the church to be efficient. Like
    any other business, you say. But a business tries to explain
    the grounds for a dismissal. They owe you that. It's good
    manners. Only the church makes such a dirty wound.
    (KINGSTON *moves uneasily again.*)
KINGSTON: Now, steady on, Lionel . . .
LIONEL: In part you see I think it's just a generalized
    impatience. I can hardly blame you. The Christian virtue
    is forbearance. It would be crazy to think it didn't take its
    toll. Yes? After a day? After a year? After fifty years?
    What do you have to show for turning the other cheek?
    What happens while you do it? What's the price?
    (SOUTHWARK *is watching him intently.*)

77

An accumulation of massive bad temper. (*Pause.*) Yes? It's only human, after all. Maybe you get to thinking, 'If I can't do this, then what can I do?'

(SOUTHWARK *is quiet.*)

SOUTHWARK: Is that how you see me?

LIONEL: You think, 'What's the point of being a bishop, being in authority, if occasionally I can't use my authority?' To whatever purpose. Your finger gets itchy. I sympathize. (*Smiles, sure of his point.*) But it's a temptation we must resist.

(LIONEL *is quiet, careful now.*)

SOUTHWARK: 'We'?

LIONEL: Why, of course. It's the same for me.

SOUTHWARK: What do you mean?

LIONEL: I'd have thought it was obvious.

(SOUTHWARK *frowns, not understanding.*)

I can go to the law.

SOUTHWARK: What?

LIONEL: Oh yes. Gilbert gave me a promise.

SOUTHWARK: Yes. I have heard that. That is hardly my fault. I am to suffer because of my suffragan's foolishness?

LIONEL: Was it foolish?

SOUTHWARK: You should have come to me.

KINGSTON: With great respect . . .

SOUTHWARK: Please Gilbert, do not intervene. Your interventions thus far have not been helpful.

(LIONEL *smiles.*)

LIONEL: It seems you have an internal administrative problem.

SOUTHWARK: I knew nothing of this promise.

LIONEL: I'm sure. But someone . . . a friend of mine has been to see a lawyer. He's advised the promise has legal status. I'm afraid you have no argument in court.

(*There's a pause.* SOUTHWARK *is disbelieving.*)

SOUTHWARK: Would you do this to me?

LIONEL: And there is a trade union.

SOUTHWARK: A what?

LIONEL: A trade union, Charlie. Remember? (*Smiles again.*) The clerical workers. They have just started a clergy section.

SOUTHWARK: That is palpably ridiculous.

LIONEL: They want a test case to prove wrongful dismissal.

SOUTHWARK: Do you have any idea what that means? Hearings? Tribunals? Appeals? Do you want to turn your whole life into a battlefield?

LIONEL: Both our lives, Charlie. Don't forget that.

(LIONEL *is quite still now.*)

No, you see, all I am telling you – I can see it's not easy for you to accept – is that at this point we are *both* subject to temptation. Equally. You in your mitre, Charlie. And me as I am.

(*There is a moment's pause. But then* SOUTHWARK *begins to speak, drawn out at last, his manner changing, his temper finally fraying.*)

SOUTHWARK: All right, very well, you want to know my reason. Why I chose you. Because you alone would dare to tell me I can do nothing about incompetence. What, I'm to be blackmailed because I'm too frightened to *fight*? (*Screams this last word with sudden emphasis.*) In any other job you'd have been fired years ago. You're a joke, Lionel. You stand in the centre of the parish like some great fat wobbly girl's blouse. Crying for humanity. And doing absolutely nothing at all.

(LIONEL *stands and stares at him, impassive.*)

Yes, I chose you. Because you are the reason the whole church is dying. Immobile. Wracked. Turned inward. Caught in a cycle of decline. Your personal integrity your only concern. Incapable of reaching out. A great vacillating pea-green half-set jelly.

(LIONEL *does not move at all.*)

LIONEL: You told me the issue was theological.

SOUTHWARK: No. It appears it's personal as well. (*Nods.*) It truly offends me, the idea that people need authority, and every time they come to ask what does the church think then they are hit in the face by a spurt of lukewarm water from a rugby bladder. And I simply will not allow it to go on.

(LIONEL *nods.* KINGSTON *watches, anxiously.*)

LIONEL: Well, that's very clear.

SOUTHWARK: There's something in your tone which is sanctimonious. You give an appearance of superiority which is wholly unearned. It's profoundly offensive. Because it is based on nothing at all. (*Nods.*) You parade your so-called humility, until it becomes a disgusting kind of pride. Yes, we can all be right if we never actually *do* anything. (*Suddenly calls out.*) My cope! (*Turns back to* LIONEL.) I want to send a message to your parish. It's a message of hope. It's to tell them the church does listen. Criteria of excellence do apply.

(*The* SERVERS *hold the robes behind him, but he does not yet climb in, suddenly quieter now.*)

SERVER: My Lord.

SOUTHWARK: You can't remember – I doubt if you read it – but in the Bible we are given an injunction. It is in my head all the time. I cannot put it out. If I could, I would sleep happy. (*Looks at him, absolutely honest now.*) Feed my sheep. That's what he told us. Feed my sheep. Feed them. (*Pause.*) And you give them nothing but your own doubt.

(*He moves back and they dress him.* LIONEL *stands alone.*)

LIONEL: I am leader of a team. That team is healthy and strong. I will leave only when they want it. Until then I am determined to stay.

(SOUTHWARK *looks at him a moment.*)

I trusted you. I trusted the Church. I still do. I still believe in it. The Church is God's instrument. Even if the bishop falls short.

(SOUTHWARK *holds out one hand.*)

SOUTHWARK: My mitre.

(*He is handed the mitre.*)

There are these moments. Today I am in a position to command a schism in the Church. If I leave the Church of England because of this heretic woman, then hundreds of thousands will follow my lead. They look to me. But I shan't. I shall stand at the brink. For a long time. All the time, shaking with anger.

(*Everyone is still.* LIONEL *watches.*)

My patience is tried beyond endurance. And by God, I shall have a victory with you.

(*He turns and sweeps out, his* SERVERS *following. There is a silence between* KINGSTON *and* LIONEL. *Then* KINGSTON *moves.*)

KINGSTON: I should follow.

LIONEL: Of course.

KINGSTON: I'm sorry.

LIONEL: No.

KINGSTON: I had no idea.

> (*A pause.*)
>
> I was shocked.
>
> (LIONEL *does not react.*)
>
> When I gave my promise I didn't realize.
>
> (LIONEL *looks at him, his rather absent manner returned.*)
>
> I still don't see.

LIONEL: Don't you?

KINGSTON: Why he chose you. Do you understand it?

LIONEL: Of course.

> (LIONEL *thinks a moment, then looks straight through*
> KINGSTON.)
>
> He chose me because he thought I would go.

SCENE NINE

*Harry's living room. It has been stripped of all ornament. The
furniture is pushed into the corners. No paintings left on the walls.
Lamps gone. It is dark except for a door leading to the bedroom, from
which light comes, and the main door, also lit, in which* LIONEL *now
stands.*

LIONEL: Harry! Harry! Where are you?

> (*He moves into the room. It is dark. Then* HARRY *appears,
> another silhouette, silently, from the bathroom.*)

HARRY: Lionel.

LIONEL: What's going on?

HARRY: How did you get in?

LIONEL: The door was open. (*A pause*) Harry?

> (HARRY *moves across to the mantelpiece and picks up an
> envelope, then goes to turn the light on.*)

HARRY: I've written you a note.

LIONEL: What do you mean?

> (HARRY *gives him the envelope.*)
>
> I came to tell you. I did what you said. I played it just as you

told me. The Bishop was outrageous.

HARRY: Good.

LIONEL: It was really exciting. I stood there. He said the most unconscionable things. He was raving. And I just let him hang himself.

HARRY: Excellent.

(*HARRY looks at* LIONEL, *quite blank, dazed.*)

Then you're all right.

(*He goes into the bedroom.* LIONEL *opens the envelope.* STREAKY *appears from the bedroom in an overcoat.*)

LIONEL: Streaky.

STREAKY: Hello, old chap.

LIONEL: Goodness, you look pale. (*Frowns at the notepaper.*) What's this?

STREAKY: Harry's leaving.

LIONEL: When? What do you mean?

(*HARRY reappears, lost.*)

HARRY: I can't find my shirts. It's so stupid. I know I put them down.

STREAKY: I'll look for you, Harry.

(*STREAKY goes into the bedroom.*)

HARRY: I've seen my Church Council. They know of my decision. I've rung round, got some preachers to cover for a while. I've done everything properly. It's odd. In four hours I did what usually takes me three months. (*Smiles.*) Just shows, eh? (*Shrugs a little.*) I thought I'd grow a moustache. Be a bit different. Then I remembered it's against Canon Law. Did you know that?

LIONEL: No.

HARRY: It's true. Do you think they're hot on Canon Law in Malta?

LIONEL: Malta?

(*HARRY looks at him, nods.*)

HARRY: A chum says I can be chaplain to the expatriate community. Baptisms, weddings, funerals. Hatch, match and dispatch, as they say. (*Shrugs.*) Well, why not? That's what we're trained for.

(*STREAKY reappears with a pile of laundered shirts.*)

STREAKY: Shirts.

82

HARRY: Thanks, Streaky. (*Looks round. There's a pause.*) I feel a bit
like Philby. My friends are taking me out.
(*Moves away, a little weepy now.*)

LIONEL: Look, what is all this?

STREAKY: There's a Sunday paper. They've been after him for
months.
(LIONEL *stops.*)

LIONEL: I didn't know.

HARRY: They're running a piece on what they call the gay mafia.
They say it's eating up the church. (*Shakes his head.*) I'm
too old. I'm sorry. Maybe if I'd been brought up differently. I
can't face the congregation. I feel I've let them down.
(LIONEL *looks round.*)

LIONEL: But this is absurd.

HARRY: I went to a party.

LIONEL: So? But what have you done?

HARRY: I haven't *done* anything. I was there. And that is enough.
(LIONEL *is about to protest, but* HARRY *cuts him off before he can
speak.*)
Lionel, for goodness' sake, don't be such an idiot. They give
knighthoods to people who publish this stuff. It isn't
coincidence. That's the country we're living in.
(LIONEL *turns, tougher now.*)

LIONEL: But it was *you* . . .

HARRY: I know.

LIONEL: It was you, good gracious, who said I had to stay and fight
the Bishop . . .

HARRY: I know.

LIONEL: It was you who was always spurring me on. You wouldn't
let me give in. You talked about the team. You said it was my
duty.
(HARRY *turns and looks at him.*)

HARRY: What, you fight the Bishop? Me fight the press? And Tony
Ferris meanwhile turn into Elmer Gantry? (*Smiles.*) Ministry
is always a balance. Well, the balance has gone.
(LIONEL *looks to* STREAKY *for help, but* STREAKY *is looking
sadly at the floor.*)

LIONEL: Harry, you're a good priest.

HARRY: I am at the moment. I have tried to be. I shall be, for an

83

hour or two more. But if I stay on, I shall not be.

LIONEL: Why? (*Looks again to* STREAKY.) I don't understand you. What would be different? We'd defend you.

HARRY: Streaky knows. I've talked to Streaky.

(*There's a silence.* HARRY's *voice is thick now and there are tears in his eyes.*)

Because I would succumb to the sin of despair.

(*After a moment,* EWAN *appears in the main doorway. He has a rucksack and a raincoat on. There is a moment's silence.*)

EWAN: All right?

HARRY: Ewan. You've got the tickets?

EWAN: Aye.

(*Nobody moves.*)

We should go.

STREAKY: Hello, Ewan.

EWAN: Good evening.

HARRY: Ewan's coming for a while. Just to see me in. Then he's coming back for an audition.

STREAKY: Well. That's jolly good news.

(HARRY *looks affectionately at* EWAN.)

HARRY: They tried to get him to rat on me. But he didn't.

EWAN: Would I?

HARRY: Never.

(*A moment's silence.* HARRY *is very emotional.*)

No. I knew that.

(*They stand a moment.*)

EWAN: Is this the lot?

HARRY: No, there's another in there.

EWAN: I'll help you with them.

(*They go out to the bedroom.* LIONEL *looks at* STREAKY, *then moves away.*)

STREAKY: How was old Charlie?

LIONEL: What?

STREAKY: Did you see him?

LIONEL: Yes.

STREAKY: Gosh, well I hope you really socked it to him.

(LIONEL *turns and looks at him, as if not hearing this.*)

LIONEL: I wonder, Streaky, has anyone mentioned the new Rector?

84

STREAKY: The new Rector?

LIONEL: Yes. If there was one, I mean. Have you heard a name?

STREAKY: Well . . . (*Pauses.*) Please, you mustn't read anything into this. I do have an inkling.

LIONEL: How?

STREAKY: Jungle telegraph.

LIONEL: It's silly, I'm feeling an idiot. If . . . I don't mean to sound selfish . . . but if, say I fight and I lose . . . if there's a new man, will you stay on?
(*There's a moment.*)

STREAKY: Look, Lionel, you know what I feel about you . . .

LIONEL: No, listen, I'm just asking.

STREAKY: You tell me. I'll go into battle. If that's what you want. I never miss a line-out. I never have. But I love this area. You know I'll fight for you, don't get me wrong. I'll fight for a while. But finally it isn't about us.

LIONEL: No.

STREAKY: It's about the people.
(*Pause.*)

LIONEL: Yes.

STREAKY: They always have to come first.
(LIONEL *nods, as the others return, carrying the bags.*)

HARRY: Streaky, goodbye. A little ignominious. Here's my key.
(*Hands it over.*) Goodbye, Lionel. We've been wonderful friends.

LIONEL: Yes. We had a good time, didn't we?

HARRY: Come to Malta. You can walk on the beach. (*Nods.
There's a pause.*) Well, we should go. We'll see you, Lionel.

LIONEL: Right.
(HARRY *and* EWAN *stand still.* HARRY *cannot move.*)
I'll see you soon.
(*Then they turn and leave.* LIONEL *takes a few paces round the empty room.* STREAKY *watches his back.*)

STREAKY: Why don't you come back to my place? I've got some old records. We could listen to Hancock. *Blood Donor*, you know. Have a glass of wine.

LIONEL: Thanks, Streaky. No, not tonight, thank you. (*Turns.*) I think I'd better go home.

Lionel's living room. HEATHER *is sitting alone playing patience at Lionel's desk.* LIONEL *comes in, carrying a small gift. It's night. The standard lamp is on.*

HEATHER: Oh goodness, I'll move out.

LIONEL: No, sit in here.

HEATHER: It's your study.

LIONEL: Well, yes. But you're welcome.

HEATHER: I'll go.

LIONEL: Don't go. (*Moves across to her.*) I bought you this.

HEATHER: What is it?

LIONEL: It's a present.

HEATHER: Thank you.

LIONEL: It's that new gardening book.

    (*She smiles at him, puts it down, goes on playing patience.*)
    I saw the Bishop.

HEATHER: Yes, of course.

    (*There is a silence. She plays on quietly.*)

LIONEL: He would like us to leave.

HEATHER: Ah yes.

    (*He looks towards her back a moment, then moves away.*)

LIONEL: I'm afraid we lose the house. We'll have to rent a flat. But that's fine. Now the family's older. We don't need very much, and we can be together.

HEATHER: Of course.

    (*He looks across at her.*)

LIONEL: It's what I've wanted, Heather. I've neglected you for so long. It's so long since we were together. (*Looks away.*) I don't know. You're suddenly sixty. What have I done with my life? (*A pause.*) They have to offer me something. They're duty bound. Perhaps a school chaplaincy. That's interesting work. With the young. I might write a book.

HEATHER: Will the flat have a garden?

LIONEL: Oh Lord, goodness. I hadn't thought. Well! (*Thinks a moment.*) We can always make do with an allotment. You see them from the railway, they always look nice.

    (*There's a pause.* HEATHER *plays on.*)

Will you . . . I wonder . . . will you come to bed with me?
(*She stops playing, her hand still over the cards.*)

HEATHER: No. It's too late.
(*She is very still, then she looks upwards, straight in front of her.*)
I've always dreamed of escaping my body. And one day I shall.
(*There is a silence. Then* LIONEL *turns away.*)

LIONEL: Now. Where are my glasses?

HEATHER: I'm sorry, darling, I'm in your way.

LIONEL: No, please.

HEATHER: But I'm out. Look. It's perfect.
(*She gestures to the cards. She's finished the game.*)
And, anyway, I'm happier alone.
(*She gets up, passes close by him, and goes to the door.*)
I'll be right by, if you need me.

LIONEL: Yes, all right. I'm just going to read.
(*She goes out.* LIONEL *at once goes over to a table and takes out a book. He sits down, without looking up, and begins to read. After a few moments he is still. Then he turns and looks directly at us.*)

SCENE ELEVEN

LIONEL *speaks into the empty air.*

LIONEL: When it goes, then it goes so quickly. It seems so substantial. Everything seems solid and real. As if what we believed protected us.
    Then you turn round and suddenly everything's gone.
(*TONY has appeared in another area of the stage.*)

TONY: It's numbers, you see. That's what it is, finally. You have to get them in. Once they're there, you can do anything. But until then you're wasting your time.
(*FRANCES appears at the other end of the area. All three are oblivious of each other. She has her coat on.*)

FRANCES: A last look round, Lord. To close the subject. Like pulling down a blind. I am going, Lord, where no one's ever heard of you. Another way of putting it, where you don't exist.

(*She smiles. There is a moment's pause.*)

TONY: It's a question of confidence. If you don't allow doubt, the wonderful thing is, you spread confidence around you.

And, for ever, so it goes on.

(LIONEL *drops to his knees.*)

LIONEL: God, you said. You gave an undertaking. Do you remember? I challenged you. Do something. Beside this silence. Begged you. Come here and help.

Do we just suffer? Is that what you want? Fight and suffer to no purpose? Yes?

Is everything loss?

(FRANCES *smiles.*)

FRANCES: I love that bit when the plane begins to climb, the ground smooths away behind you, the buildings, the hills. Then the white patches. The vision gets bleary. The cloud becomes a hard shelf. The land is still there. But all you see is white and the horizon.

And then you turn and head towards the sun.

(*The stage darkens.*)